HAUNTED FLORENCE

H.P. BRADLEY

Haunted America

Published by Haunted America
A Division of The History Press
Charleston, SC
www.historypress.com

Front cover: Red Doe Plantation. *Courtesy of the* Florence Morning News.

First published 2018

Manufactured in the United States

ISBN 9781467139052

Library of Congress Control Number: 2018942444

Dedicated to
all lifelong learners who transform and grow and embrace the unknown with courage and wisdom to inspire and to enlighten…

CONTENTS

What is, is not; and, what is not, is…
—The Trickster

PREFACE

As a professional educator and writer, I continue to have a passionate interest in developing meaningful curricula that will engage, excite and inspire students to become lifelong learners. I have a graduate degree in exceptional education and an undergraduate degree in psychology with a specialty in opening the door of academic learning again for students who have lost interest in learning or no longer really believe that they can learn at all. I am very pleased to have the opportunity to have my first nonfiction book, *Haunted Florence*, included in the Haunted America series because I believe that this series does make learning about American history meaningful, engaging, exciting and inspiring for learners of all ages. Like most lifelong learners, I also have an inquisitive desire to want to know more about history and the supernatural and paranormal to further understand the deeper meaning of life. My life experience has convinced me that to truly understand human psychology is to understand the full dimension of who we are as living souls who do have an existence beyond this physical world.

ACKNOWLEDGEMENTS

I would like to give special thanks to Jennifer Reyna, a librarian with the E.N. Ziegler South Carolina History Room at the Florence County Library, and Don Kausler Jr., regional editor of the *Florence Morning News*. They both helped me with gathering together the missing pieces of historical information and photos that were needed to make this book complete. I would also like to thank my father and mother, Don and Sharon Bradley, two lifelong learners whose passion for learning, history, photography, reading and writing significantly inspired me and also encouraged me to inspire and enlighten others to become lifelong learners as well.

Introduction

In this book you will come to know Florentine spirits and ghosts from all walks of life, from the most supernatural to the most human, from the most diabolical to the most divine, from the most joyful to the most disturbed, from the poorest to the wealthiest, from the most intelligent to the most foolish and everywhere in between. Their life stories also share the amazing collective story of what it means to be American and live in what has become the great and diverse nation of the United States of America from the very beginning as a vast landscape of rugged and treacherous wilderness to the modern high-tech age of the twenty-first century today. Whatever you may discover at the timeless crossroads of haunted Florence, you will be encouraged and inspired to want to learn even more about the fascinating history of the Magic City and also reconsider what it means to be a ghost…

1
BECOMING FLORENCE

Florence began as a railroad depot at the juncture of three rail lines in 1852: the North Eastern Railroad, the Cheraw and Darlington Railroad—both running north and south—and the newly formed Wilmington and Manchester Railroad, running east and west. Making Florence the intersecting crossroads of these three railroads was the vision of General William Wallace Harllee. He obtained the charter for the Wilmington and Manchester Railroad in 1846 while serving in the South Carolina House of Representatives.

Born on July 29, 1812, Harllee had already distinguished himself in his early military career as a major of Harllee's Battalion, Charleston Militia in 1836. He was later commissioned as a major general of the fourth division, South Carolina Militia in 1845. William Harllee also practiced law in Marion, Florence and Darlington and was admitted to the South Carolina bar in 1833. He was to become president of the South Carolina bar in 1886. Continuing his political career as lieutenant governor of South Carolina, he was a signer of the Ordinance of Secession in 1861. Harllee was one of the largest planters in the state as well until his death in 1897.

The exact location of this frontier depot named Florence is considered to be on what is now called Hoffmeyer Road, nearby to where the Florence Mall is today. Florence was named after Florence Harllee, born on July 2, 1848, the first daughter of William Wallace Harllee and Martha Shackleford Harllee. William Harllee named his first daughter Florence after the heroine of the novel *Dombey and Son* by Charles Dickens, which was published in the same year of Florence's birth. Florence had three older brothers and two younger sisters.

The City of Florence stayed very busy during the Civil War by transporting troops, artillery and supplies. The Florence railroad depot and the railroads in the area were the main target of Union general Sherman's attack. A Confederate train conductor spotted the Union soldiers before they arrived in 1865 and was able to give enough warning to spare Florence from certain destruction. The Confederate soldiers were then able to successfully defend against this Union attack. Traveling south from Cheraw, Sherman's rampage of war still led to the destruction of nine years of railroad construction in three days. Hundreds of miles of railroad tracks around the Florence area were torn up and melted to be wrapped around trees, infamously referred to as "Sherman Neckties."

Florence's life began in a grand style, even surviving the Civil War without too much trouble. The City of Florence was chartered in 1871, with a rapid enough increase in population to cause a housing shortage and included many refugees who moved to Florence from Charleston after the Civil War. However, in 1873, Florence Harllee's good fortune dramatically changed when her beloved plantation, Sunnyside, was burned to the ground. Florence even left her namesake town to move to Marion during this time.

Florence and her sister Lizzie returned to live in Florence in 1889, one year before Florence was officially incorporated as a city. Florence and her sister Lizzie never married, choosing to share expenses instead and live together as financially independent women. They also chose to become schoolteachers during this time and endeavored in two small businesses together selling spices, flavorings and cloth. Florence later became the first librarian of the City of Florence in 1903, when the library was moved to the city hall. Sensing that her death was near after becoming very ill from influenza, she made funeral arrangements to spend one night in her beloved St. John's Episcopal Church on Dargan Street before she was buried at Hopewell Cemetery in 1927. Hopewell Cemetery is listed in the National Register of Historic Places.

And yet, this humble railroad depot that had been named Florence still remained, first built in the rugged expanse of what was still a part of Darlington County in 1852, about ten miles south of the city of Darlington, built in the countryside of a remote pine forest as a rough board shelter and the only stop for passengers to get off and on the train in Florence. Ebenezer Church and a hotel at the Sleepy Hollow Plantation of C.A. Dargan offered nearby accommodations for travelers who might choose entertainment and rest at the Sleepy Hollow Hotel. Perhaps the iconic ghost story "The Legend of Sleepy Hollow" by Washington Irving, published in 1820, was Dargan's personal inspiration for choosing this name for his plantation and hotel.

Ebenezer Church at Jeffries Creek opened its doors in 1778 and was founded by Evan Pugh and Richard Furman. Timothy Dargan II, born in 1743 in Virginia, was an early minister of this church who served until his death in 1783. Charles A. Dargan, his grandson, born on August 14, 1825, and passing on in 1861, would only begin to see the transformation of his rural and rugged plantation landscape to officially become incorporated into the bustling City of Florence in 1890.

The City of Florence experienced heightened interest in education and arts during the 1920s and 1930s. Henry Edwards Davis, a well-known Florence attorney who was also on the Board of School Commissioners, advocated for an even more public library in 1920 that did not require a membership ticket to access. In 1925, the new library was completed in honor of the veterans of World War I. This newly constructed library building is an excellent example of the Neoclassical Revival architecture with Beaux-Arts influences and is listed in the National Register. The architectural design was the work of the Florence architecture firm Wilkins and Hopkins, with William J. Wilkins and Frank V. Hopkins as its principals.

The Florence Public Library grew to become the Florence County Public Library in 1964. In 2004, the Florence County Public Library moved to its new location from Irby Street to Dargan Street and is now called the Drs. Bruce and Lee Foundation Library. Dr. John Bruce and Dr. Frank Lee formed this philanthropic foundation in 1995 to help to continue to improve the quality of life in the Florence area through supporting human services: health, medical, education, arts, religion and the preservation and promotion of cultural, environmental and historical resources.

The Drs. Bruce and Lee Foundation also was responsible for building the new Florence Little Theatre on Dargan Street in 2008. The original theater group, the Community Players, began performing in 1923, part of Florence's renaissance of the 1920s. The group soon changed its name to the Pinewood Players when that club offered a building for performances in the Five Points area. Unfortunately, this building burned down, requiring the performers to seek another location. The theater group was without a home of its own for quite some time, requiring performances be given outdoors, in school and community auditoriums, supportive Florentine residents' backyards and even a garage. It was not until 1947 that the Florence Little Theatre found another home of its own in a small movie house that had previously been a part of the Florence Army Air Base. This air base was abandoned after World War II. Then, in 1968, the Florence Little Theatre broke ground for its own building on Cashua Drive, where it remained until 2008.

With World War II came the peak time for rail traffic. Now, busy highways have also been added, continuing to make it possible for Florence to flourish as a timeless crossroads into the twenty-first century, blending most of its original seven streets—Dargan, Evans, Front, Irby, McQueen, Coit and Cheves Streets—to the more recent Florence Harllee Boulevard. Florence is a midway point between Miami and New York as well as between Washington, D.C., and Orlando, offering a unique crossroads for travelers and tourists to choose to stop in and visit along their journey. Florence has been called a retail hub of the Pee Dee Region because it is also midway between Columbia and Myrtle Beach and boasts the Magnolia Mall, the largest shopping mall between these two cities.

On the city streets of Florence, both old and new, there are many abandoned homes and buildings that linger on and, along with them, reputations that tell stories of times gone by. These stories have helped to shape the very fabric of Florence just as the railroad tracks have, carrying with them their own cargo of memories. The land also remains, with perhaps only the bones left of a house that had once existed there before. Perhaps you might find the stone pieces of a house's foundation or even the charred embers of lumber that has suffered through the tragedy of a fire. You may find a few scattered personal belongings or utility items that have been left behind.

Whatever may be found, Florence is still very rich with American heritage that continues to live and breathe today within the timeless crossroads of this growing city, still containing within it people from the wealthiest to the most impoverished, from the most educated to the most illiterate, from the most liberated to the most enslaved, from the most enlightened to the most ignorant. Who are the people of Florence? The same people who founded this city close to 170 years ago, along with the many people who came after. They stayed and had children who stayed to have their own children and so on, continuing to become more of a part of what the City of Florence is and will become. Many others will just end up passing through this timeless crossroads as they travel from one point to the next. Those who come to Florence and stay believe that Florence is their destined home. There also are many Florentines who will choose to remain in Florence, even after they have passed through physical death to the other side, still not quite ready to move on…

2

Timeless Crossroads

The sounds of trains rumbling down the tracks can be heard throughout Florence at any given moment of the day. Even now, what would have seemed to have become obsolete by the twenty-first century is still very much a part of the fabric of this multifaceted tapestry called Florence. A younger sister city of Charleston, Florence has many forgotten memories and hidden secrets it can share, yarns that it can weave; the past, present and future are bound together in the realm of the supernatural and the paranormal. Living souls are here among those who still walk in the flesh—the souls of those who have departed physically, yet remain.

Why these living souls remain becomes one of life's great mysteries. Growing paranormal research continues to confirm the presence of living souls as ghosts here among us. Those who seek to understand why respectfully, humbly and without fear often do, as they gather all of the clues together that these living souls still have to offer.

Many have time to prepare before they leave their physical bodies, and some are forced to leave abruptly, without any warning. We will meet one such ghostly family murdered in the darkness of night, caught in the nightmare of this kind of terrible and shocking surprise. Members of this family never had a chance to really say goodbye before they could no longer return in the flesh. It is quite understandable then why there are some living souls like these who might have great difficulty adjusting to such a traumatic transition as being without a physical body.

Why would such an existence even be allowed? To be effectively trapped between two worlds, no longer able to walk in the flesh but unable to completely rise above this world? And yet, those who appear trapped in this way are still able to communicate with those who are really listening and paying attention. For those who have been so gifted, awareness of the supernatural is a reality that they cannot completely ignore. Why this might be also remains one of life's great mysteries, a mystery that remains completely unfathomable for most.

These clues from the physically departed may be physical objects that they have left behind. One daughter of another family who is included in this book left behind many objects in her home of what she desired others to find without ever leaving a note to explain, perhaps hoping that those who found these objects would understand her cryptic message. Other clues may come in the form of hearing sounds or even voices, sometimes with the ability to see who is speaking and sometimes not. Although no one has claimed to see her ghost, this same daughter has been heard warning those who dare to enter her abandoned home to not cross over into the kitchen area next to her mother's bedroom.

Sometimes these clues may be in the form of becoming a watcher of a surreal silent movie, where you can often see someone acting out a scene that has great personal significance for them. One ghostly couple in Florence appears to be searching for something that they have lost while continuing to stay on at an abandoned boardinghouse. Although this window is boarded up now, they can sometimes be seen through an upper-story window in the early morning hour of the sunrise. A man in overalls and a long-sleeved shirt appears to be standing over a woman who is wearing an early turn-of-the-twentieth-century dress and is on her hands and knees, frantically searching for something on the floor.

Many times, these surreal scenes are the re-creation of physical death. Are these living souls seeking some kind of justice? They are almost always very disgruntled by the turn of events that led to their own physical deaths. Are they seeking vengeance or retribution? Are they attempting to make someone else pay through the pain and suffering that they felt at the end of their physical life? Such dark energy can often attract other spiritual entities that are not human, like the Trickster of the Native American Pee Dee legends who sometimes likes to haunt in swampy areas. These spiritual entities have their own axe to grind about why they are trapped between the spiritual and physical planes against their will. These spiritual entities can sometimes become attached to humans, making them dangerous and potentially harmful to others, as these living souls have chosen or been chosen to combine their spiritual energy with these unholy spiritual entities, which are much more powerful than they are.

Sometimes the desire for justice may be for the purpose of protecting others from suffering the way that they were made to suffer because the person who offended them so grievously is still able to harm others. They may feel obligated to attempt to stop them because of the knowledge that they now possess. Sometimes such noble human souls can attract good spiritual entities that are not human and are more powerful than they are to aid them in accomplishing their mission, carrying them up to the higher spiritual plane when their mission has been accomplished.

Perhaps it is regret that causes a living soul to not be at peace enough to leave the physical world behind, even though they really no longer belong in it. So filled with sorrow, their souls have become too heavy to rise above and embrace the next phase of their existence. These living souls may often be seeking solace or comfort, empathy or forgiveness, seeking the understanding that they must have to finally bring the peace that is needed. The air may become haunted and very heavy at dusk, so heavy that a misty cloud might surround you around the area of a railroad crossing in Florence that is spotlighted in this book. So thick is the air that is so filled with sorrow and regret that one can cut it with a knife.

Sometimes it is fear that keeps living souls bound to the physical plane, the fear of letting go and embracing the unknown, preferring instead to hold on to at least what is still known and familiar to them, even if it is an empty existence that no longer fulfills. They know beyond a shadow of a doubt that they do not belong in the physical world anymore, but they are not ready to let go. They may wander aimlessly to and fro, sometimes in a heightened state of anxiety, compelled to do what they still refuse to do to make their souls free to rise.

And perhaps it is the love of the physical world or people who still remain in it that makes it so difficult for a living soul to completely let go. Perhaps it is the sentimental affection of a beloved home or piece of land, a workplace or a school, a favorite restaurant, theater, museum and so on. There is one ghost who you will meet in this book that has such an affection for a beloved plantation that he greets visitors on the front steps and offers tours.

For some ghosts, their desire to remain attached to a particular location is more sinister than sentimental. For these souls, their need is to possess and keep what they believe is still theirs so that no one else can have it. "Mine" is their vain and covetous refrain that has prevented them from crossing over to their next spiritual destination. One such imposing figure of an elderly woman in a black shroud who threatens any would-be intruder with a cane can sometimes be seen menacingly peering through the upstairs bedroom window of her home, warning all to beware and keep out.

Sometimes the scenes that might be acted out for you at the supernatural cinema are intense moments of joy and ecstasy, triumph and success, great pleasure and comfort. Smells or even tastes have been shared as extrasensory communication so that another might be able to appreciate their experiences even more intensely. There is the living soul of a very dedicated worker you may see who still walks to work to a now abandoned tobacco barn dressed in work pants, a work shirt and work boots. You may even smell the acrid scent of a cigarette burning, an offensive odor to many, but not for this ghost, who may have found working and smoking to be some of life's greatest pleasures. He still enjoys them even after he has passed through death.

These living souls have become so attached to their physical life in this world that they cannot imagine why they should ever have to leave it. They cannot imagine what could possibly be better than what they have already enjoyed here on earth. So why should they let go? In one Florence home, you can sometimes hear the haunting notes of someone playing a timeless piano tune from beyond, even though there has been no piano in the home for quite some time. It might even be another person that a living soul cannot risk being apart from, even for a moment, because of the doubt that they may not ever see this person again if they let go of this physical world.

There are many reasons and clues that might help to explain why a living soul would remain in this world spiritually even though it has already physically departed. The more important question may become what are you, if anything, supposed to do about it? In this book, you will find a mosaic imprint of some of the spirits and living souls who have departed but still remain to further understand their personal life and experience and also further understand how these experiences reveal the truth of the American tapestry of Florence and all those who have lived within its borders. In Florence, the lumbering trains still carry their cargo back and forth down the railroads of yesteryear, blaring their horns to make sure that they are still heard and providing as useful a function as they did when they were first made to serve the timeless crossroads.

3

The Trickster Near Francis Marion Road

Florence was built on a series of swamps that are all a part of the northeastern corner of South Carolina, known as the Pee Dee region, which includes the Pee Dee River. Pee Dee, meaning "something good," is named after the Pee Dee Native American tribe. Native Americans lived in harmony with the lands that would become South Carolina for thousands of years before the first Europeans arrived.

The Native Americans were willing to move as needed to successfully adapt to these changing lands in order to provide the way for their continued survival. They respected nature so much that they personalized their relationship by naming different aspects of nature and attributing to these entities different personalities, emotions, intellects and purposes, even to the point of worshipping nature. Native Americans viewed all living creatures and aspects of nature as equal to or even greater than themselves.

For example, a tree is not lumber; a tree has a living spirit that is sacred. Sap is not syrup; it is the blood that seeps from the tree when the tree has been cut. Animals are not resources to be shackled, contained, controlled, mistreated, tortured and recklessly killed by the will of men. Animals are living beings that deserve to remain undomesticated and treated with the same dignity and respect that we might be willing to give to another human being. The taking of an animal life is only justified by the need to survive, with all proper thanksgiving and with all proper recognition for the sacrifice of the life that has been lost. The land itself must be nurtured like a baby to keep the soil good and ensure the survival of all. The Native Americans lived by the creed that if they took care of the land and all of its living creatures, then they would continue to be taken care of.

Archaeological evidence seems to indicate that Native Americans originally came from Siberia, traveling across the Great Land Bridge, along with many animal and plant species, to the pristine new lands of the Americas. Sea levels dropped as much as sixty-five feet during the massive freeze of the ice age, revealing solid ground to travel on to their next destination. Archaeological evidence also seems to indicate that many Native Americans of South Carolina lived inland, near rivers like the Pee Dee and adjacent to flood plain swamps.

The Trickster became known in Native American myths as a supernatural entity that sometimes haunts swampy lands. All were warned to be cautious when approaching such lands, for the land itself seemed to be filled with the foreboding essence of trickery, shifting and changing at will to appear solid when it was not. Mists form and rise from the murky waters, obscuring the light of the sun, making these swampy areas feel very gloomy, sickly and dismal. Ignoring the warning to beware of the Trickster could even lead to your death, if you were not careful. Considered neither evil nor good, the Trickster offered the magical balance of transformation—what is, is not and what is not, is. One form that may rise from the mists is that of a childless swamp creature, a ghostly mother who lives in the marshy land and mournfully cries for all of her lost children. Any mortal who dares to try to follow these wailing cries to their source will surely die. Some say that this maternal swamp monster is malevolent, deliberately luring children to their deaths, while others say that her intention is not to harm but to warn.

The Pee Dee were some of the first Native Americans that Europeans ever met while exploring the Americas. Spanish explorer D'Allyon first met the Pee Dee in 1521. The Pee Dee Indians welcomed the British colonists and even came to their aid against the Tuscarora in 1711 and the Yemassee in 1715. The Pee Dee also helped in peace negotiations. In 1717, a Pee Dee named Tom West traveled to Charleston to negotiate peace between the British and the Charraw tribe. Apparently, the peace was short-lived, and the conflict began again.

The Pee Dee joined forces with other Native Americans to help American colonists defeat the British during the American Revolution. It was during this time that an American colonist named Francis Marion became known as the Swamp Fox. The Revolutionary War had not been going well for the American colonists of South Carolina. Charleston was captured by the British in 1780. The American colonists then suffered another crushing defeat in Camden soon after. As a result, the now frail Brigadier General Marion, who walked with a limp, was forced to flee into the swampland of the Pee Dee backcountry with a ragged band of followers.

Perhaps Marion met the Trickster in this region, for he soon began to manifest all of this supernatural entity's attributes, earning him the Swamp Fox moniker. The fox is another well-known form that the Trickster may take in Native American culture. So inspired, Marion mounted a devastating campaign of guerrilla warfare in the final years of the War of Independence that turned the tide of the war against the British. Often completely surrounded by his enemies, the Swamp Fox specialized in the surprise tactic of ambush. He would swiftly attack and then disappear just as quickly back into the swamps. The Swamp Fox's courage and reputation for outsmarting his enemies brought more and more newly inspired volunteers to join him. British officers became distracted by and then obsessed with capturing the Swamp Fox and his troops. After many attempts to do so, one British lieutenant colonel named Banastre Tarleton remarked, "Let us go back…as for this damned old fox, the Devil himself could not catch him."

Haunted swamplands of the Trickster as seen from afar. *Author's collection.*

By the early 1800s, the remaining Pee Dee Indians lived in small family clans along the Pee Dee River. Some archaeologists and historians believed that all of the Pee Dee Indians had perished or been assimilated into the Catawba tribe in 1808. However, the Pee Dee tribe of South Carolina is still alive and well. This distinct tribe of Native Americans was officially recognized again by the State of South Carolina in 2006. The Pee Dee continue to help their tribe and surrounding communities to improve their quality of life.

Most of the swamplands in the Florence area have been well drained for quite some time, becoming forests in the twenty-first century. The swampy areas that remain are often hidden due to the tall trees that shield these bogs from view and help keep their secrets. The same warning resounds as loudly as when the words were first spoken by mortal men: "Beware of the Trickster" when approaching these swamplands, for what is, is not and what is not, is.

There is a swampy area near Francis Marion Road in Florence that has developed a reputation for being haunted. Most people have understandably avoided crossing the outer tree line or going deeper into the center of its swampy maze, for it is impossible to see more than a few feet ahead of you at a time. Dark shadows can be seen lurking among the trees, sometimes remaining stationary and sometimes seemingly moving of their own volition. Strange mists, revealing faces that do not appear to be completely human, have also been described as rising from the center of this swampy maze. Is the Trickster still here in Florence? Some people believe so, and most would not dare to go where they might meet with it, unless motivated to do so out of certain desperation.

4

A COONSKIN CAP

It was during the 1830s that the popularity of the coonskin cap grew alongside a wellspring of romantic patriotism. Just as "The Star-Spangled Banner" was a patriotic song to sing, the coonskin cap was the patriotic fashion of choice for many Americans, including South Carolinians who traveled through the swampy lands of the Pee Dee region. Even elite South Carolina aristocrats were inspired to wear the coonskin cap during the 1830s. A man named Hugh Legare, a planter and Whig politician, would often shrewdly wear a coonskin cap while campaigning to increase his popularity, especially when traveling from Charleston to the more rural areas of South Carolina, such as parts of the Pee Dee that would later be transformed into Florence. Legare knew just how powerfully symbolic this popular fashion accessory had become.

Perhaps the Trickster even gave its seal of approval as well, because the raccoon is yet another guise that the Trickster may choose for its physical form in the Native American tradition. The coonskin cap is a hat that is made from the hide of a raccoon, a fashion that originated with the Native Americans. This raccoon cap came to symbolize all of the rugged independence, clever inspiration, divine intervention and amazing strength of will that had been required for the United States of America to become its own recognized country—no longer controlled by Great Britain and the first democracy that the world had ever known.

When traveling through Florence today, you will not see the many tall trees and swampy remote landscapes that still existed in the area during

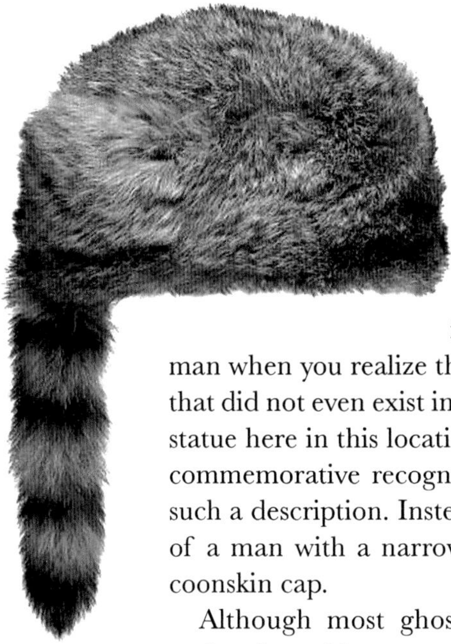
A coonskin cap. *Google Images.*

the 1830s. What you may see though, if you choose to travel down the western end of Pine Street, is the abstract appearance of a man who remains on this thoroughfare as a patriotic and nostalgic reminder of this American time gone by. You may even begin to feel disoriented and eerily caught in time after seeing this mystical man when you realize that you are traveling down a street that did not even exist in the 1830s. There is not a sculpted statue here in this location or some other physical kind of commemorative recognition that you might expect from such a description. Instead, there is the phantasmal figure of a man with a narrow, hawkish face who is wearing a coonskin cap.

Although most ghost sightings have only described seeing the sudden appearance of a partial apparition, with the head and upper torso of this particular ghost peering out from behind a single tree, some psychically sensitive observers have witnessed a more complete surreal scene of the entire landscape. The view shifts to what it must have been like in the early 1830s, a vision of what this outdoorsman must have seen. A few of these extraordinary observers have even reported hearing birds chirping and cawing and other sounds of wildlife moving through the swampy lands of this historical time. However, no one has reported hearing this ghost ever attempt to communicate with anyone in any way. No one has described him as ever moving, either. Instead, all sightings have described him as remaining still, fixed and motionless. Could this be some kind of a paranormal clue as to the ultimate fate of this silent statuesque ghost, or is he just unable to speak or move in this form?

No one has claimed to know for sure though who this man was or what his spiritual purpose might be for haunting this specific location. Did this man die here? Did some terrible fate befall him? Does he still have an important personal message to communicate to us even after death? Or did his own personal life become a much greater message after death? Perhaps he chose to become a symbolic touchstone of remembrance—like the

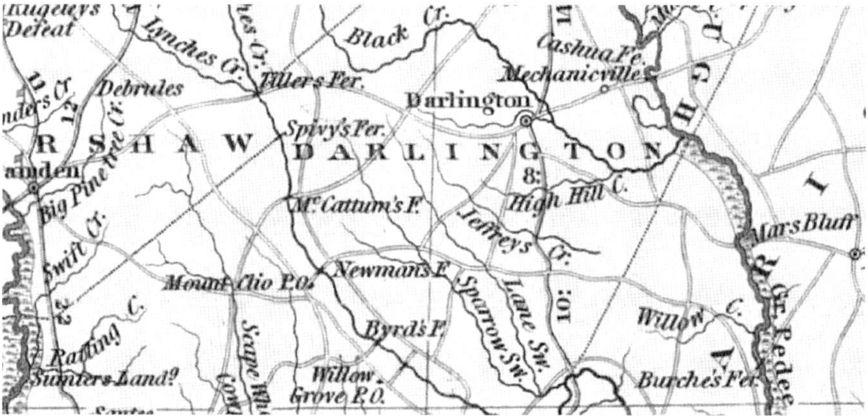

Map of the Pee Dee region of South Carolina in the early 1830s. *Courtesy of Sciway Maps.*

coonskin cap itself—of passionate patriotism and romantic nostalgia for a time in the United States of America when no dream seemed impossible to transform into reality, even the birthing of a new nation into this world. This nation continues to endure and successfully transform through every test of time.

The most popular local legend of this capped ghost is an adventurous and rather gruesome tale that does help answer some of these questions. This unsettling account of local legend begins when this ghost was still quite rugged and solid and walked in the flesh. The seemingly fearless adventurer in question had chosen to travel alone through the Pee Dee region on what would become his most fateful journey. He was traveling south from the northern Darlington area of South Carolina and is believed to have been helping to scout out this area of the Pee Dee for future development. The area officially became Florence approximately two decades later. He was traveling on foot and was very well skilled in survival. However, neither his survival skills nor his coonskin cap could protect him when death waited in this peculiarly precarious and perilous swampland of supernatural entities, wild beasts and pine trees.

Before arriving on what would become Pine Street in 1898, approximately seventy years later, this brave and well-seasoned scout encountered no significant dangers or obstacles as he traveled by Jeffries Creek. He had also made all of the necessary preparations and had all of the basic supplies to live off the land as needed while he continued along on his journey. He even had weapons to protect himself, a knife and a gun, and, one could surmise, enough faith and courage to believe that he could overcome any challenge. But could he overcome death? Or did it even matter to him if he did?

For many adventurers who chose to be explorers and scouts, the risk of tempting and daring death to take them was a significant part of the thrill and excitement that often motivated them to continue to go on more and more daring adventures. However, part of what gave them this grave courage was that it really did not matter to them if they lived or if they died from one moment to the next. What did matter a great deal to them was dying a heroic death—one worthy to be remembered—with their sense of honor intact.

Of course, for other scouts and explorers, their motivation was much more pragmatic than emotional. They were seeking profit far more than any fame or honor that their successful wilderness adventures might bring. Perhaps this South Carolina scout was of this type, and his trip to what would become Florence was intended to be much more routine and uneventful for him rather than drama-filled and thrilling. Those who told this local legend believed that he had probably made a scouting trip to this area of the Pee Dee at least once before that had proved uneventful, and this experience made him overly confident that there would be no trouble this time either.

According to local legend, this scout was dead wrong. He became increasingly convinced, with ever growing anxiety and alarm, that he was being followed by someone or something that was stalking him. The scout knew the stalker must be dangerous, and he became sure it meant him harm the closer that he got to his destination. He began to seek cover among the trees to see if he could get a good eye on what might be following him. This discomfited scout began to move as carefully and cautiously as he possibly could from tree to tree to distance himself from where he had first begun to hear the stealthy predatory movements of whatever wild creature or person had decided to make him the object of intense focus. The air then grew strangely still and quiet, and he could no longer hear any sounds or movement at all. Still anticipating a possible attack from behind, he turned around to look for what would prove to be the last time, as the savage predator was now right in front of him. The vicious attacker then chose this opportune moment to end this unfortunate scout's life.

Most Florentines who shared this tragic tale believed that it was a bobcat that attacked this outwitted man and made him its prey on that awful day. However, there were a few who were convinced that what attacked him was more supernatural than fur. Most of these same locals still believed in the myth of the Trickster, a supernatural entity who never offers its loyalty to any mere mortal, even to one who wears a coonskin cap.

5

Welcome to Red Doe Plantation

There have been many ghost stories and hauntings surrounding Red Doe Plantation over the passing of close to two centuries. Such phenomena are not surprising when one considers all of the people who have lived, worked or visited at this location during such a relatively lengthy span of time. Red Doe Plantation is located in the Mars Bluff community of Florence. Mars Bluff—formerly spelled Marr's Bluff during the Revolutionary War—is a region in the northeast corner of South Carolina that is adjacent to the Great Pee Dee River and was later included as a part of Florence. This change in spelling, however seemingly insignificant, was indeed significant after all, because this spelling error completely changed the meaning of the name. *Marr* is an old Norse word considered extremely rare in its usage that refers to a habitation near water, or a marsh. The word *mar* or *to mar* means to damage or to spoil.

The word *mar* takes on a disturbingly spooky meaning when one considers the local Florence legend of a wolfish looking man with a claw for one of his hands who curses anyone he is able to reach with this same monstrous claw. This twisted man's ghost has been seen by a very frightened few. It appears to rise from the hedges and shrubbery that cover the side entrance of Red Doe when people approach. It has been described as having large, elongated, glowing eyes and a mouth filled with snarling teeth. It is rumored that the wolfish man's right hand became disfigured by a curse; lustful and wicked desires of perverse evil consumed his life as they consumed his tormented soul. Some say that this vile man was a groundkeeper who molested any

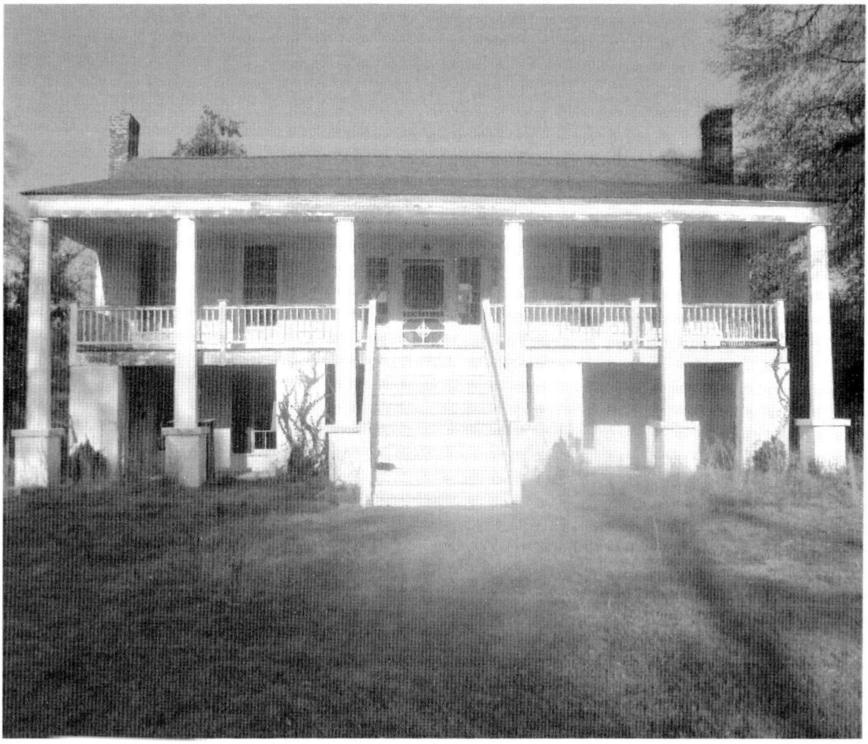

Welcome to Red Doe Plantation. *Author's collection.*

children that he could seduce and lure into his terrible snare during the 1960s. Most believe, however, that he became associated with Red Doe Plantation much earlier, during the Civil War era, and he became cursed by slaves there after he repeatedly attempted to molest their children. A few believe that this beastly groundkeeper's sexual perversions were not directed toward children but animals and he committed disgusting acts of bestiality with dogs. Legend has it anyone who is unfortunate enough to be marked by this wolfish man's terrible claw will surely suffer the same fate and be consumed by their own perverse and wicked lusts.

The name Mars, without the apostrophe, changes the meaning again and seems to refer to the red planet. A strange event occurred on March 11, 1958, that lent this new meaning more credence, as a Mars-like crater formed from the accidental deployment of an atomic bomb in the Mars Bluff community. Fortunately, this atomic bomb did not cause devastating destruction because the fissile nuclear core had not yet been installed. This community now retains the dubious distinction of being the only area in the United States of America to have ever had an atomic bomb dropped on it. By the 1970s, some people had begun to believe that this bombing incident was the reason for the Mars Bluff name. The crater site from the bombing was recognized with a state historical marker fifty years later, in 2008. However, this site remains on private property, technically making all would-be visitors trespassers unless they have been given explicit permission to go and see this site for themselves. While the community was spared the worst, some damage did occur that directly affected the Gregg family. At the time, three little girls—Helen and Frances Gregg and their cousin Ella Davies—were playing inside a playhouse in the woods built by Walter Gregg, the owner of the property that was bombed. All three girls were injured, as were Walter, his wife, Effie, and their son, Walter Jr. The playhouse was destroyed along with many nearby buildings.

The seeds of Red Doe Plantation can be traced back to this same Gregg family and Ireland, close to 150 years before the plantation was conceived in the Mars Bluff community that would become a part of Florence. A man named David McGregor, born in 1700 in Belfast, Ireland, married a woman named Jannet Baxter and had five children: Hugh, Henry, John, Joseph and Jannet. David McGregor did not make the journey to South Carolina himself, but three of his sons did: Henry, Joseph and John.

Although they were born in Belfast, Hugh, Joseph and John met their deaths in various parts of South Carolina. Hugh (1725–1793) died in Williamsburg County; John (1732–1775) died in the Old Cheraw District, which become a part of Florence County; Joseph (1742–1824) died in either Willow Creek, which is in Marion County, or the Evergreen area, later a part of Florence County. It is uncertain when the three brothers decided to change their family name from McGregor to Gregg or exactly what their reasons were for doing so, but it was a common choice for many people to symbolize beginning a new life in a new country.

John Gregg married a woman named Eleanor Conn and had five children: Margaret, Mary, Jannet, Robert and William. John moved to the Jeffries Creek area of Marr's Bluff between 1754 and 1760; during that time, his first daughters, Margaret and Mary, were born. John Gregg married a second time and had two sons, John Jr. and James. The genealogical record of David McGregor becomes less clear at this point, but it is believed that James married Elizabeth Wilson and had nine children: Jannet, Mary, Sarah, Margaret, John, David, James, Elias and John. In 1800, John Gregg (III) married Jannet Bigham—who apparently was his niece—daughter of

Margaret Gregg and William Bigham. John and Jannet Gregg had eight children: Eliza, Ezra, David, Sarah E. (who died at age five) Mary, Sarah A., John Eli and Evander.

John Eli Gregg was born on January 28, 1805, and died on June 15, 1873, in the Mars Bluff community of Florence. Eli Gregg inherited the Gregg Plantation from his father, John, in 1836. Eli Gregg also is significant in Florence's history because it was he who sold 750 acres of land to General William Harllee in 1852. It was this land that the railroad depot named Florence was built upon, the depot that became Florence's cornerstone. Sallie Gregg Wallace and her husband, Joseph Wilds Wallace, became owners of the Gregg Plantation in 1920, almost a century later. Their plantation home was destroyed by fire in the early 1920s and was rebuilt in 1924. Two slave houses from the pre-1830 era of the Gregg Plantation are listed in the National Register. The Gregg Plantation is a part of Francis Marion University today. In 1961, the Wallace family donated 100 acres of land for the foundation of what was first called the University of South Carolina at Florence. In 1970, Governor Robert McNair changed the school's name to Francis Marion College, and the college achieved the status of university in 1992.

What about Red Doe Plantation? Listed in the National Register of Historic Places, Red Doe Plantation became the Gregg Plantation's next-door neighbor in 1846. Red Doe Plantation was built by Eli Gregg's younger brother Evander. Evander was born in the Mars Bluff community on July 8, 1818, and he began the construction of Red Doe in 1836—at the age of eighteen—a vision that took him approximately ten years to complete. In its formation, this estate included approximately one thousand acres of land. Robert Legare Singletary acquired Red Doe Plantation from Evander in 1867, two years after the end of the Civil War and a few years before Evander's death in 1874.

Some Florentines who visited Red Doe have described seeing Confederate soldiers standing outside around a flagpole on this property when lightning strikes. Evander Gregg would have been the owner of this estate during the Civil War. Was this meeting a part of the emergency effort to rally a defense against General Sherman and the Union soldiers who were rapidly approaching? Another haunting that a few empathetically gifted visitors to Red Doe have imparted was the dreadful experience of a slave girl who may have lived in one of the slave cabins that are still there behind the plantation. Approach one particular slave cabin and open the door, and you may still hear her desperate, disembodied cry: "Please ma'am, don't let him hurt me!"

Red Doe changed hands through Sarah Evans Singletary, the widow of Robert Legare Singletary, who sold this plantation to Sarah Gregg Wallace and Joseph Wilds Wallace in 1912, before the Gregg family acquired the Gregg Plantation in 1920. In 1934, one of Wallace's sons, Joseph Wilds Wallace Jr., named the place Red Doe after the horse of Andrew Hunter, an American Revolutionary rider. Perhaps, in the darkening days of the Great Depression, this son was seeking to inspire and rekindle the courage and hope of the American spirit to triumph again. Joseph Wilds Wallace Jr. had a brother named Marion Chisolm Wallace; they were the great-grandnephews of Evander Gregg. Marion took up his family gauntlet in 1940 and restored Red Doe. It is believed that this man and his family lived at Red Doe for the longest period of time, through the 1980s.

It is unclear what happened to Red Doe after the loss of Marion Chisolm Wallace. At some point, a man named Robert Pearce Wilkins acquired Red Doe and donated this estate to the Pee Dee Rifles Organization and the Sons of Confederate Veterans Camp in 2006, a partnership that became Red Doe Plantation Inc. that same year. The original vision for Red Doe Plantation Inc. was for this plantation to become a museum. However, there was little funding to support this project. Then, after five years of determined effort, Red Doe Plantation Inc. was awarded an enhancement grant from the South Carolina Department of Transportation for approximately $100,000 toward the restoration of Red Doe in 2013. This crucial first step toward restoring Red Doe, after close to seventy-five years, was completed in 2014. The restoration effort made a significant improvement toward restabilizing this home and made it more structurally sound.

Other paranormal sightings reveal malevolent spirits at Red Doe—shadowy figures that can sometimes be seen staring out from every window, as if watching and waiting to seek who they may harm. These sightings were noted by witnesses to have started at the turn of the twenty-first century, approximately ten years after Red Doe became vacant and then virtually abandoned. It is uncertain if the timing of this new century is significant in any way to this paranormal occurrence. However, a few witnesses believe that these malevolent spirits may be the lost souls of slaves who are still seeking vengeance after death for whatever injustices and torments they may have suffered.

Red Doe Plantation Inc. and the Florence City–County Historical Commission partnered with the Palmetto Trust for Historic Preservation to put Red Doe Plantation back on the market. The Palmetto Trust for

Historic Preservation is a nonprofit organization that formed in 1990 for the purpose of preserving and protecting the historic structures of South Carolina. Red Doe Plantation was listed for sale for a modest $150,000 in June 2017, with a preservation easement by the Palmetto Trust that would require the new owner to complete the restoration process of this structure as either a private residence or a commercial business. This plantation quickly sold within two months.

Another ghost sighting by visitors that is much more welcoming than malevolent is the occasional appearance of a middle-aged red-headed man in denim jeans and a denim shirt. He may choose to greet you, should you decide to come to Red Doe. He is most often seen on the grand front steps, as if he were there waiting for you. No one knows for sure who this ghostly tour guide is. Whoever he may be, he certainly believes that he is still needed and must be responsible for Red Doe—even from beyond the grave—to ensure that it will be well taken care of again.

6

THE VOODOO WOMAN OF FIRETOWER ROAD

What is a fire tower, and what was its purpose? Fire towers served a very important function as lookout posts that could be staffed to warn of wildfires that had begun to blaze in the area before they began to burn out of control. As the towers are no longer needed in the twenty-first century with the advent of satellite technology, many cities struggle with deciding what to do with these obsolete pieces of history. Should they be preserved or just torn down? There was a fire tower in the Mars Bluff community of Florence that remained active before being removed and dismantled by 2012. Firetower Road is located in the Mars Bluff community and was likely so named to recognize this fire tower.

Why would a woman living on Firetower Road become known as the "Voodoo Woman?" And why does she still haunt the area today? One must understand the history of slaves in the Florence area to even begin to answer these questions.

Most people think of slaves from Africa when they think of slaves. However, there was a significant intermediate stop between Africa and North America: the West Indies, including the country of Haiti. Those who have any knowledge of Haitian culture or of the voodoo religion are aware that it is from Haiti that voodoo developed, with roots in West Africa. Therefore, it does not seem like such a stretch of imagination that the Voodoo Woman was a slave at some point who learned voodoo as a part of her cultural heritage. If she had been a slave, who might have brought her to South Carolina and when? What events later in life led her to be able to move into her own home in Florence?

The Pee Dee region was a bloodthirsty, wild, rugged, remote and isolated frontier for the first Welsh settlers who came to settle these lands in the 1730s. Bloodsucking insects of many kinds that incessantly attacked the other inhabitants of these lands for most of the year seemed to symbolize this gnawing hunger for blood. There was no law or order. Crime was pervasive in the settlement. This time in Pee Dee history for these first settlers was described on the history page for Florence County as idle and immoral; they spent their days drinking, hunting, shooting, racing, gambling, "with every aspect of wickedness, even swapping wives and children like cattle and horses, more rude than even the savages around us." The first record of any slaves in the Pee Dee area was in 1748, approximately twenty years later.

By 1757, the number of slaves had reached about 500, with a total population of 4,300 in the Pee Dee area. About 25 percent of the population owned slaves, with slaveowners having an average of three or four slaves. There also were Native Americans who might have been included in this settler population. Many Pee Dee, classified as "Settlement Indians," began cohabiting with the Anglos in the 1740s as an alternative to joining the more powerful Catawba tribe. Some of these Settlement Indians became slave owners, too.

In the thirty years since the first Welsh settlers arrived, one of the most daunting challenges had been the process of draining the swamps to gain more farmland. Many of these settlers now saw themselves as colonists, privileged land owners rather than wild pioneers. These settlers had become lumberjacks, ranchers and planters of indigo.

The American Revolution ended the British bounty for indigo as a cash crop. Local farmers were searching for an alternative. The invention of the cotton gin by Eli Whitney in 1793 provided the answer: cotton. Planting cotton led to a rapid rise in the slave population and a dramatic shift in lifestyle for many in the Pee Dee region who became slave plantation owners. These plantation owners continued to heavily invest in draining the swamps so that they would have more usable land and be able to keep their slaves. Slaves often chose to escape from the plantations by crossing through these swampy areas and taking refuge there. By 1850, just two years before the Florence railroad depot was built, the number of slaves outnumbered the number of free men in what would soon officially become Florence County. The most likely possibility for how the Voodoo Woman arrived in South Carolina is that her parents were brought to the United States by one of the many privateer slave trading ships that regularly traveled back and forth from the West Indies to Charleston and she was born in the states.

A decade later, the Civil War brought dramatic change again. With the Emancipation Proclamation of 1863, the day of reckoning had come for the slave–plantation owner lifestyle. Abraham Lincoln, the president of the United States, proclaimed that "all persons held as slaves are, and henceforward shall be free." The ultimate Union victory immortalized these words in all of the blood that was shed and through all of the lives that were lost during this time of war. This lifestyle of moral confusion that had been justified by the arrogance and pride of greed had come to its end. Most slaves continued to work on plantations during the Civil War. Many slaves fled north or joined the Union army when it became clear that they were free. However, not all former slaves were willing or able to make such a dramatic change.

U.S. census records from 1870 and 1880 noted that one particular girl, about thirteen years old, named Francis Drew was living with the Pinckney family during this period. The 1870 census listed her occupation as "Domish School," but these words were barely legible. Is it possible that what had been written was Donnish School instead? *Donnish* is a word used to describe someone who is too scholarly, too serious or overly intellectual, like a stereotypical professor. Was this a clever or even a sarcastic play on words to describe this former slave girl's new occupation after the Civil War? At twenty-three years old, this former slave girl's name appeared to have been changed in the 1880 U.S. census record. If so, why? Her occupation was listed as servant/cook. Why would a former slave choose to then go by the name of Kate Pinkney later in life when she moved to Florence?

There was a Kate Pinckney who was the daughter of Dr. Charles Cotesworth Pinckney and Mary Ryan Pinckney and would have been living with this former slave girl. Are Kate Pinkney and Kate Pinckney actually the same person? Or did this former slave girl decide to take this name on as her own after she became a free woman? If so, why? If the woman who became Kate Pinkney was in fact the former slave girl in the earlier census records, then she would have been approximately seventy-three years old in 1940.

Kate Pinkney, who later became known as the Voodoo Woman, moved into her newly built home on Firetower Road in 1940. Pinkney was not living alone; Kate's daughter, Atleene Pinkney, lived with her. Atleene Pinkney was born in 1912, making her twenty-eight years old in 1940. Apparently, Atleene was Kate's only child. However, it would seem impossible that Kate could be Atleene's biological mother, for in 1912, Kate would have been fifty-five years old. Was Atleene adopted by Kate? Atleene never had any biological children of her own either but was called a surrogate mother by many children in Florence. She also taught middle school for many years and was known as a devout Christian who regularly attended church and studied the Bible.

Kate and Atleene grew cotton and tobacco during the 1940s. Kate also developed a reputation in the neighborhood for practicing voodoo. People said that she could summon demonic entities through voodoo dolls and could actually talk to the devil, but she would have to give it something in return, even human souls. People who knew this family well knew that Atleene was very against her mother's voodoo practice, but she was never able to persuade her mother to change her beliefs before her mother passed on.

When you walk inside Kate and Atleene's deteriorating and decaying two-bedroom home and stand in the hallway, you may see that the first bedroom has furniture in it, a four-poster bed and a child's bed at the foot of it, about the size of a toddler bed. Why would there be a child-sized bed in a home with two adult women who had no young children? The second bedroom is partially barricaded and farther back in the house, right next to the kitchen. The only other room is a living room with a couch in it.

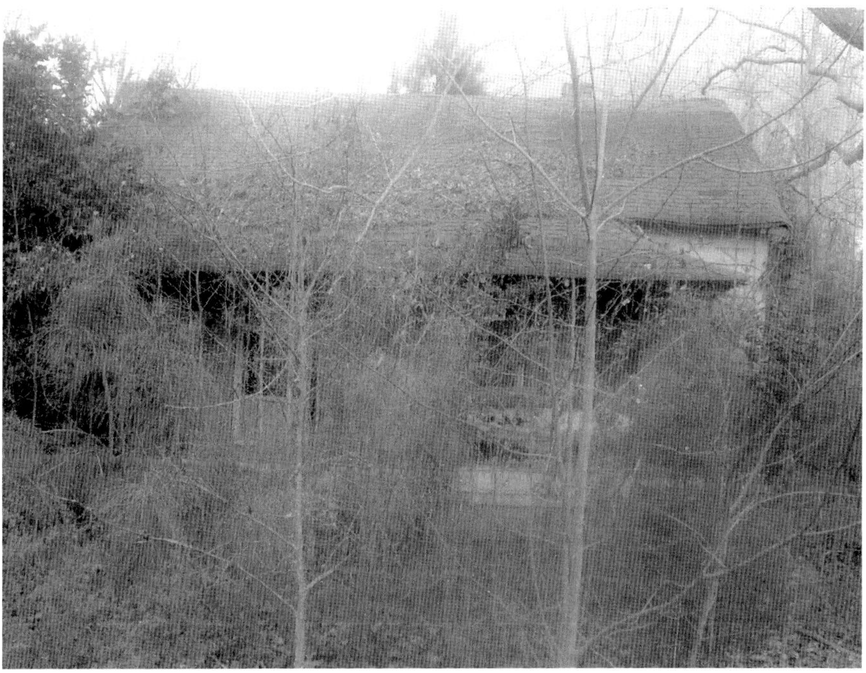

A house of voodoo. *Author's collection.*

The hallway bookcase is still filled with books, including many copies of the Bible, in different translations.

Although no one has ever claimed to have actually seen the ghost of Kate or Atleene, in one paranormal sighting, there was the manifestation of an elderly woman's face that an observer believed was probably Kate's on the corner of the living room couch. This surreal face appeared to continue to age right before this extrasensory observer's eyes until it had become so ancient and brittle that it started to crack open, with what seemed to be occultic markings of lines. The design began to extend diagonally on either side of this face and became distinctly diamond shaped. This new face wore an elaborate headdress of some kind that arched up around the top of the head and was crowned by a circular sphere. Did this paranormal sighting reveal the voodoo *loa* (spirit) that Kate favored or favored her?

Other paranormal occurrences at this location convinced a neighbor that even the trees themselves were haunted by voodoo spirits. There is a large, towering tree that has shiny white bark with crooked tree limbs growing at the right corner of the property when facing the front door. The psychically intuitive neighbor believed that this imposing tree is the actual home of the voodoo loa attached to Kate, and the loa travels back and forth through the tree limbs to the roof and then inside Kate and Atleene's home. He also believed that the trees that are growing in front of the home were deliberately positioned there to stand guard and deter unwanted visitors, with branches that reach out of their own volition to scratch and maim those who attempt to cross to the front door or part to reveal an unhindered path for those who are welcomed. This neighbor claimed to have had both a welcoming and unwelcoming experience, with a welcoming experience the first time and an unwelcoming experience the second time—resulting in deep scratches on his arms from shielding his face and eyes from the attacks of these possessed trees. He never went back to the house again after being unwelcomed.

Although the haunted experiences of the voodoo face and trees were unique to those extrasensory observers, most who know of Kate and Atleene believe for sure that their living souls remain at their decaying home as ghostly Florentines. If you dare to walk inside this haunted home and step foot into the kitchen, an unseen voice may be heard giving warning to you to not go any further, a voice that has been heard by more than one visitor. Is Atleene warning others to stay away from the center of where her mother practiced voodoo? It is uncertain when Kate left her physical body in death. Atleene passed on in 2008, quite possibly the last resident to live there before this home became abandoned.

7
A DEDICATED WORKER

Tobacco became known as the "Pearl of the Pee Dee" in the mid-1890s, replacing the royalty of cotton as a seemingly more egalitarian crop that many farmers could grow for more modest profits. By 1900, the Pee Dee region had become the center of Bright Leaf tobacco production for South Carolina, with 95 percent of the crop acreage planted here. The Pee Dee area had the right kind of soil for tobacco to grow. Many efforts had been made to grow tobacco in other regions of South Carolina, but the soil proved to not have the right mix of sandy clay subsoil. Therefore, cotton continued to be king in the rest of South Carolina, even when planting this crop was no longer as desirable or profitable. There is one local ghost story from rural Florence of a dedicated worker whose ghost has been sighted in more than one location and for whom tobacco became the pearl of both his financial freedom and his great personal satisfaction.

The first tobacco warehouse auction in South Carolina was in Florence in 1890, the same year that Florence officially incorporated as a city. Organized by Frank Rodgers at his Florence Tobacco Manufacturing and Warehouse Company, this first auction had all of the buzz and excitement of an important social event. Many Florentines saw this warehouse and those that would follow as proof of their city's increased progress and prosperity. In 1884, the City of Florence had a thriving business district before ever being officially incorporated. By 1903, Florence had grown from just seven streets to over twenty-one streets, approximately tripling its physical footprint in about twenty years of time. Florence boasted of being a hub of the Atlantic

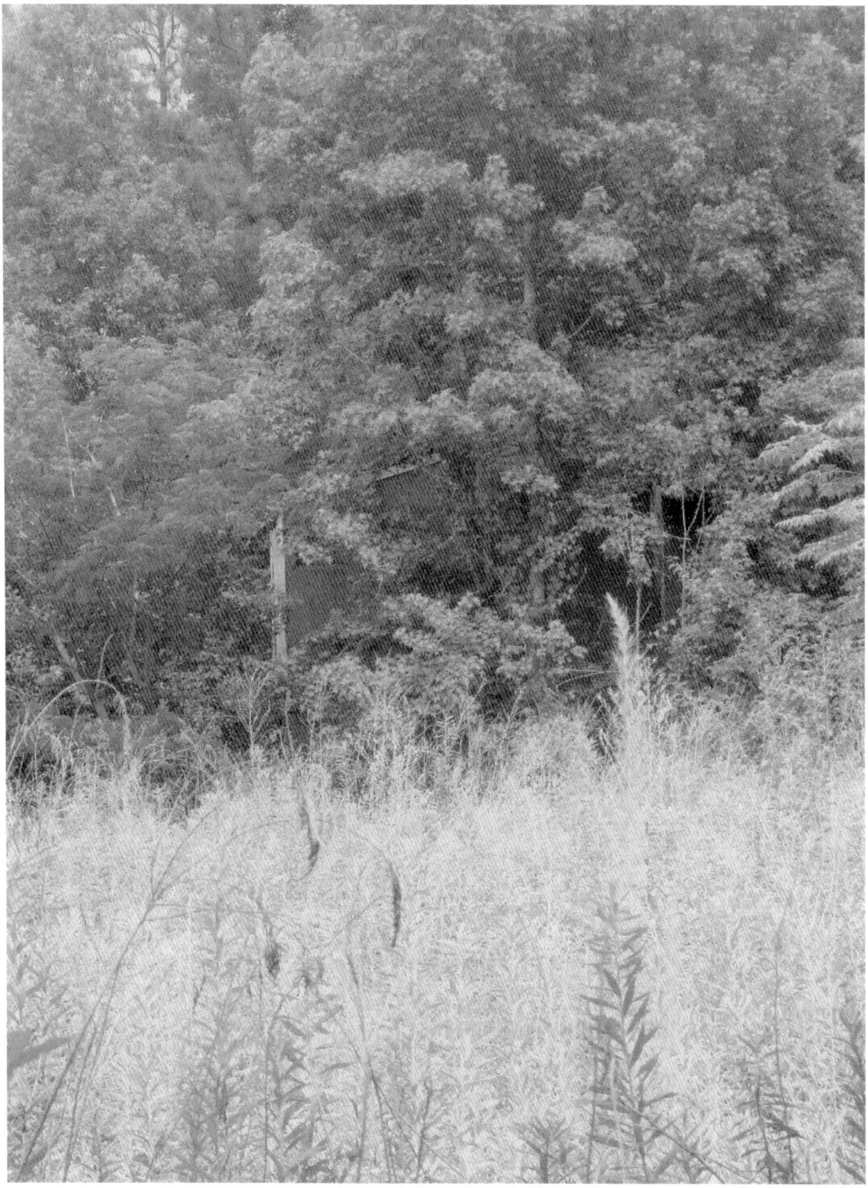

A tobacco barn peeking through the greenery. *Author's collection.*

Coastline Railroad and a branch of the Southern Cotton Oil Company, with many manufacturing industries, including ice, candy, baskets and crates, a bottling works, a waterworks, a printing company, a newspaper, a library, an opera house, a bank, stores, specialty goods and services shops and offices, hotels, a city hall, the county courthouse, a public school, numerous churches—including a Catholic convent—and the CA Gregory Tobacco Company, along with several more tobacco warehouses.

Many changes also were taking place in the more rural communities of Florence like Mars Bluff during this post–Civil War period. The misguided economic royalty of enriching a very few by enslaving others with cotton cash and the grand illusion of Dixie's plantation life had been replaced with the emancipation promise of sharecropping tobacco. Unfortunately, sharecropping did not make it possible for former slaves to completely unshackle themselves from former plantation owners who had split their plantation lands into many smaller farms in order to continue to prosper. Unable to buy land themselves and reap the full profit of their own labor, former slaves remained at the mercy of these landowners to decide how fair they wanted to be with what they would give in return for sharecropper labor. By the early twentieth century, nearly 70 percent of all white farmers in the South owned their own land compared to only 6.5 percent of black farmers. Laboring under a new form of servitude, these sharecroppers never earned a monetary wage to buy into the growing economy of Florence. Essentially, all they worked for was to have only the most basic of necessities like food, clothing, rent for a shack to live in and rent for the tools and supplies that they needed to continue to farm the land. The outlook was bleak for these sharecroppers; they would never have the freedom of choice that money provides to decide how they and their families might be able to grow past indentured servitude to invest in and prosper from all of the opportunities around them in their expanding city. The extreme impoverishment of the sharecroppers and their families became another world away again from the wealthy tobacco manufacturers and tobacco warehouse owners. These new elites replaced the former plantation slave owners in the twentieth-century agrarian economy of Florence.

The outlook was so bleak, particularly for southern black farmers in the early twentieth century, that it is amazing to fathom the strength of will and profound faith that it must have taken to still believe that they could really ever be free enough to embrace the words of the Emancipation Proclamation and live with full self-determination. One of the few who had found a way to do just that was a former slave named Ervin James.

James bought approximately 250 acres of land in the Mars Bluff area of Florence in 1870 from Eli McKissick and Mary Poston. He then founded the community of Jamestown. His vision and passionate desire was to see that former slaves be able to live independently, free of any debt or ownership by another man, beginning with his own family. What it must have been like, what a glorious moment it must have been for Ervin James to make that land purchase just two years before his death in 1872. He became, through his descendants, like a twentieth-century Underground Railroad train conductor, a former slave who was able to lead his family and future descendants and other former slaves and their families and future descendants out of economic bondage to freedom, one by one.

Jamestown residents, who worked for thirty to sixty cents a day farming and doing strenuous labor, were paid modest wages. However, even earning less than a dollar a day was much better than earning no money at all. Now, residents of Jamestown were empowered to have the real freedom of choice that money could buy. Many Jamestown residents chose to move on after finding their financial footing to even better work conditions and economic opportunities in other parts of the country. Jamestown flourished as its own community in the Florence area for seventy years, until 1940. Ervin James's descendants and other families in the area continued to purchase additional land. These Jamestown residents grew into a community of about 250 people during this time. In 2006, the Jamestown Reunion Committee erected a historical marker celebrating the settlement. One original Jamestown cabin remains, and there are ongoing plans for its full restoration.

The Jamestown Foundation is dedicated to this restoration effort. This foundation has opened Jamestown to the public in order to provide the opportunity to experience what life was like in the Jamestown community. Ervin James's descendants still gather together every year for a reunion, having begun this tradition, called Come Celebrate Jamestown Reunion, in 1988. Different events that are offered during this celebration include historical reenactments, Gullah storytelling, basket weaving, corn husking, furniture making, net casting, indigo dyeing, iron working and more.

Reunions sometimes include other people than expected; the virtually unseen, who no longer walk in the flesh, may also choose to join in the celebration. Some rural Florence residents believed that there is one African American man who gained his financial freedom in Jamestown for the first time and still lives in the area even after death to continue to joyfully celebrate and remember his remarkable success. He is believed to have been able to go on to purchase land himself in the Jamestown

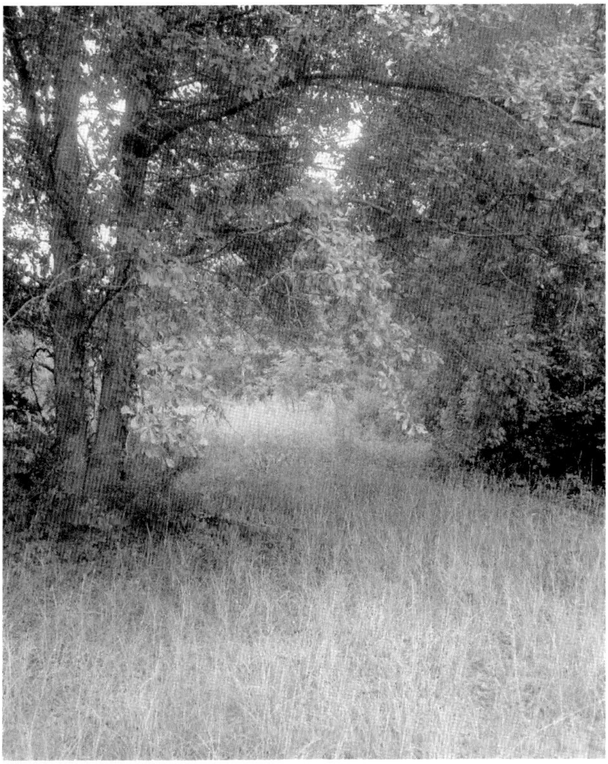

The path of a dedicated worker. *Author's collection.*

area during the 1940s and then mostly utilized his land for the purpose of growing tobacco. No one is certain today who this man is, but one Florence resident has claimed to have seen his ghost appear more than once at the Jamestown reunion, dressed in outdoor work clothes with a cap on his head. This smiling ghost appears for only a few moments near the northern tree line of the crowded lawn and then disappears.

The Jamestown area of Florence remains rural today, even into the twenty-first century. When traveling through this area, you may be able to see an old dilapidated tobacco barn peeking out through the trees. This structure is believed to be the tobacco barn of this same African American resident that at least one person has claimed to have seen at the Jamestown reunion. When you begin to focus on this tobacco barn, you will see a path through the trees and greenery that leads directly to it.

Florentines in the neighborhood believe they have seen this ghostly African American man still walking on this path to his shrouded tobacco barn. The most common ghost sighting is a man in his thirties or forties wearing outdoor work clothes and boots. He is tall, lean and smiling, walks

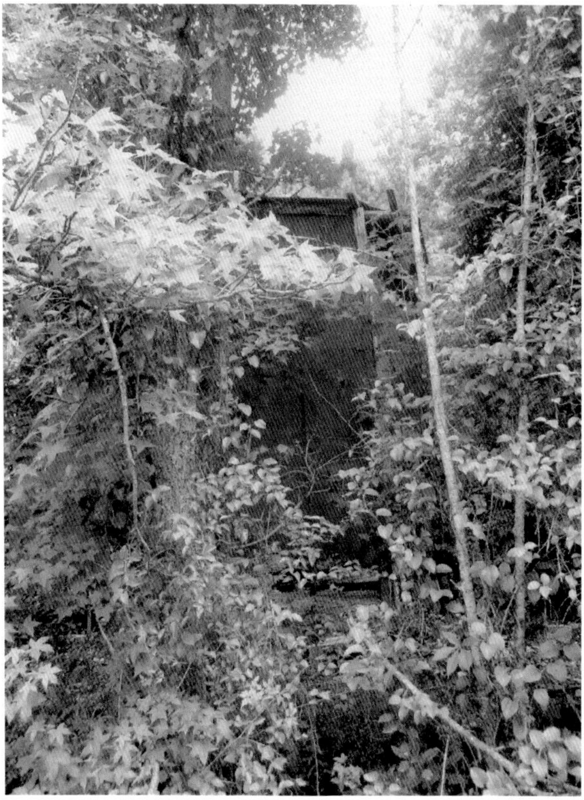

The tobacco barn of a dedicated worker. *Author's collection.*

with a jaunty determined step and holds a burning cigarette in his hand. Some have even been able to smell the acrid scent of his smoke as he passes by. His apparition can be seen fading into the distance as he gets close to the tobacco barn and then disappears.

Another Florentine neighbor has described seeing the surreal appearance of this same smiling man walking on the path, but he is holding the hand of a little boy instead of a cigarette. The little boy is wearing similar work clothing like the man and has a cap on his head. The little boy is about six or seven years old, and he is carrying a ball in his hand. Is this little boy his son?

And, who is this dedicated worker, who still walks to work, even after death? Did he know the descendants of Ervin James? Was he able to buy his own land, too? If so, that would certainly explain his exuberant happiness at a time that was still very bleak for far too many. Quite possibly—from the great personal satisfaction of working and being a father to the simple pleasure of smoking a cigarette—this living soul still enjoys fond memories, even from beyond death.

8

THE WATCHERS AT THE CORNER OF GAILLARD STREET

The Florence Stockade and the Florence National Cemetery have become known for being haunted by the lost souls of Civil War soldiers who are still traumatized from their horrific ordeal and have therefore been unable to move on to their next spiritual destination. The Florence Stockade, also called the Confederate States Military Prison, began operations in September 1864 but was closed five months later, in part due to the horrific and inhumane conditions that the Union soldiers who were detained there were forced to endure. During this time, it has been recorded that close to three thousand Union soldiers died out of the eighteen thousand who were imprisoned there. Lieutenant Thomas Barrett oversaw this prison and was known for his cruel behavior, including murdering prisoners. One can only imagine the level of anger, frustration and even rage that Confederate soldiers like Barrett may have been feeling as they sensed that their defeat was so close at hand. In April 1865, just two months after this prison was shut down, the Civil War was over.

The Florence Stockade is located off of National Cemetery Road on Stockade Road and is approximately one mile south from what is now the corner of Pine and Gaillard Streets. It's likely Gaillard Street was named after Peter Gaillard, a Confederate officer who was captured at the Battle of Weldon Railroad in 1864. Gaillard Street became a part of Florence in 1893. It is ironically poignant that this street might be named after Gaillard, who was captured and then later escaped himself. Union soldier or Confederate soldier? In the darkness of night, and especially without a uniform on, would

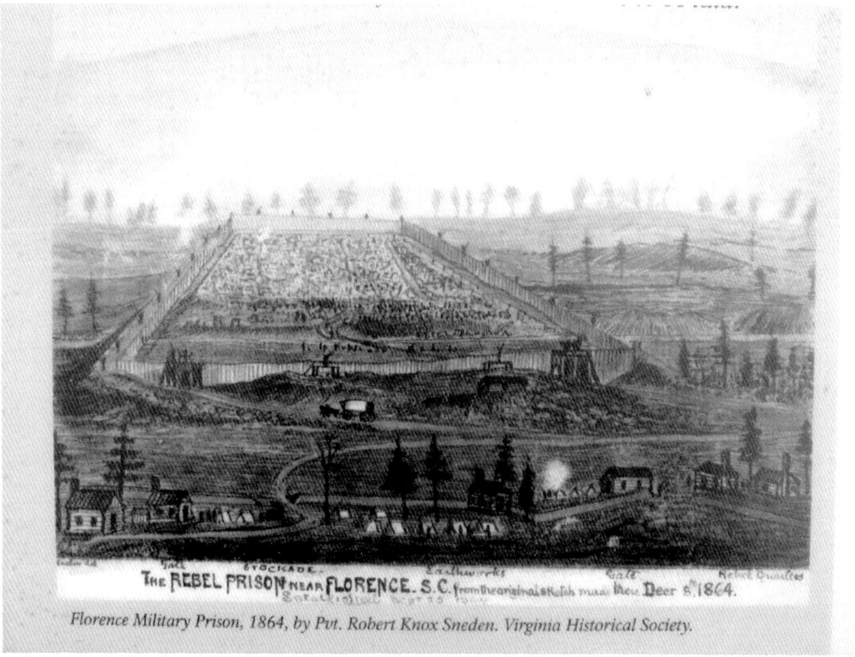

Private Robert Knox Sneden's artistic rendering of the Florence Stockade. *Author's collection.*

anyone really be able to distinguish between these prisoners of war who shared such a traumatic experience? The Florence Stockade was listed in the National Register in 1980. This stockade is open to the public and is a part of the City of Florence Trail System. The Friends of the Florence Stockade and the City of Florence offer a walking tour of this historical site.

How many Union soldiers may have attempted to escape their hellish suffering in this prison? Deep trenches encircled this stockade, with a "dead line" established approximately ten to twelve feet away to discourage many prisoners from even trying. A dead line is the outer edge of a prison where prisoners could be shot and killed if they escape across it. What was waiting for any who might have made it that far beyond the timber wall? A forest of trees and swampland that they could only desperately hope would provide the necessary cover to make their escape.

The Florence National Cemetery is located approximately a quarter of a mile from the Florence Stockade. This site was designated as a National Cemetery in 1865 for Union soldiers who had perished while being imprisoned in the Florence Stockade and who had previously been hastily buried in trench graves. Remains of Civil War soldiers were also reported to have been transferred from other nearby burial sites to this new location. The Florence National Cemetery was listed in the National Register in 1998.

At least one extrasensory visitor to the Florence Stockade has witnessed the ghostly appearance of the tortured soul of a Union soldier who seems to be reliving the last moments of his own agonizing death. The figure attempts to stand up and rise again from an area of trench that is still visible from the wooded walking trail. His apparition was described as being very thin and emaciated, with what looked like open sores on his face. Was this man mistakenly buried alive? Or did he attempt a daring yet desperate and ultimately fatal escape for freedom? Quite sadly, he is still trapped in this awful prison even now, without the sweet release of even death to free him.

Some visitors to the Florence National Cemetery have claimed to have seen multiple spirit orbs hovering above the grave markers there. Two of the largest orbs have been seen traveling rapidly back and forth across this space in a curious crisscross formation while intersecting with the paths of each other. It is uncertain what the spiritual significance might be of this crisscross formation, but witnesses believe that the orbs are the souls of two

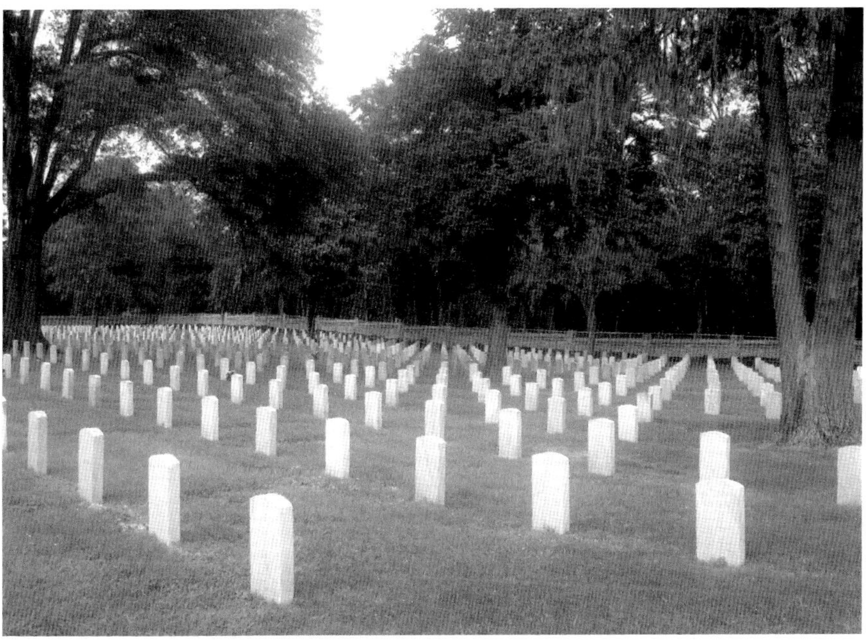

A cemetery of remembrance at the Florence Stockade. *Author's collection.*

of the lost soldiers at this site who still have not found peace in death, despite the honorable effort of those seeking to give them a proper burial.

In 1905, forty years after the Civil War ended, though ghostly spirits still remained, there were no longer trees in the swampland beyond the dead line. Instead, Pine and Gaillard Streets intersected there. Mr. Sulzbacher was a prosperous jeweler in Florence who built his Queen Anne–style home on this corner that year. The Queen Anne style became quite popular among the wealthy elite in the United States during the 1880s through the early twentieth century. This architectural style was known for being eclectic and included such features as steeply pitched irregular rooftops, partial or full width porches and occasional turrets and towers. There was indeed a tower included in the construction of Sulzbacher's home. It is uncertain whether or not this tower was actually used as a physical watchtower by him or others or if it was merely there for decorative flair. It is also uncertain what year Sulzbacher arrived in Florence, but he probably came to the United States along with a great wave of other immigrants who arrived in New York City between the years of 1882 and 1910.

Sulzbacher was Jewish and likely moved to Florence from New York City. It also is likely that he experienced some prejudice and stigmatization for being Jewish and perhaps was even viewed with suspicion because his culture and ways were different than the mainstream southern culture—but Sulzbacher had money to help protect him from the most brutal forms of prejudicial hatred. However, it is doubtful that he was ever fully accepted into the society of the Florentine elite, despite his display of status. There were opportunities to connect in the Florence community with other Jews, though: they formed an elite society to ease any sense of social isolation and rejection from the mainstream. One such Jewish society was called the Florence Hebrew Benevolent Association, founded in 1887 to "unite the Hebrews of Florence and surrounding country into a fraternal and benevolent association to assist needy Israelites." Sulzbacher was a member of this association. In 1912, the Florence Hebrew Benevolent Association became the Beth Israel Congregation and is still active today, also drawing members from nearby Darlington, Dillon and Marion and as far away as Laurinburg, North Carolina. Less exclusive, the Jewish-owned Jacobi Hotel on Front Street opened its doors for business in the early 1890s and became known for offering comfortable accommodations to the weary train traveler. It is very possible that the Jacobi Hotel was the first stop for Sulzbacher in Florence and he spent many comfortable nights there before building his own home on the corner of Gaillard Street.

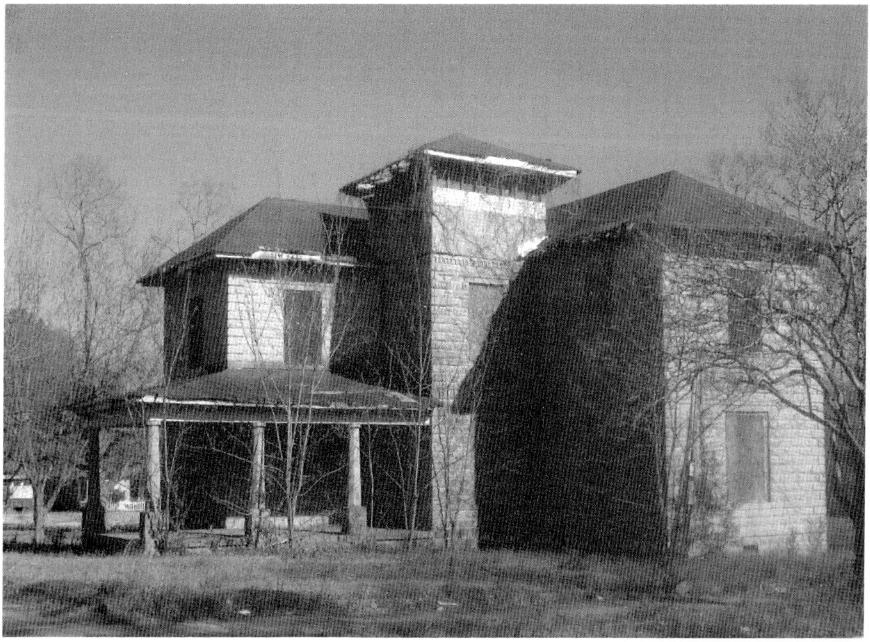

We watch from the corner of Gaillard Street. *Author's collection.*

The corner of Pine and Gaillard Streets is seemingly abandoned and neglected today, with Sulzbacher's home in great need of renovation. However abandoned and neglected this corner may appear to be, if you go to this corner and walk around the perimeter of Sulzbacher's home, you may begin to have the distinct feeling that you are being watched, a feeling that may overwhelm you. Even when walking on Gaillard Street, you may find your eyes being drawn up to the tower, searching for a face or for any movement, but you might not see anyone there, at least not anyone in the flesh. There are a few Florentines who are sure that they have seen the apparition of an elderly man watching from the roof of this tower when they were walking down the sidewalk of Gaillard Street. One Florence resident described seeing this same elderly ghost when walking on a shortcut path through the backyard of this home and further described this ghost to have been wearing a suit. Is this apparition the ghost of Mr. Sulzbacher?

And what new horrors may have taken place beyond the Florence Stockade for those who did manage to escape approximately one mile north past the dead line, to what is now the location of Mr. Sulzbacher's home, only to be recaptured? It has been said that this corner of Gaillard Street is also haunted with the lost souls of soldiers who never found peace within after their traumatic experiences during the Civil War. Are these lost souls the watchers at the corner of Gaillard Street? Or is Mr. Sulzbacher still keeping an eye on his property and maybe even his neighborhood from the other side? Or are these watchers all of the above?

9

BURNED

Abandoned homes could burn for emotional, physical or financial reasons—and there is one more reason to consider. The supernatural cannot be ruled out as another possibility when spirits can manifest and even become fire starters themselves. There is one abandoned home near the corner of Gaillard and Pine Streets that suddenly began to burn in the early hours of one wintry morning with no explanation. The fire continued to burn for close to two hours before it was contained, causing significant damage to this home and exposing its interior.

An extreme example of burning for emotional reasons was during the Reconstruction period of the 1870s. Spirits were low for those who could not let go of the so-called glory days of Dixie, admit that they were morally wrong and just move on. Burning embers remained in the South, crackling just beneath the surface, of intense hatred and resentment over what many white southerners believed was the sore loss of their honor, dignity and self-respect from their defeat in the Civil War. They may have even believed that the new freedom given to former slaves was at the direct personal expense of their own self-determination. They refused to change and accept the new Yankee ways of thinking. They refused to embrace the technological progress and transformation of American society through the turning of the twentieth century with open arms. Many white southerners also felt shocked, disconnected, disoriented, confused, ashamed and lost in their world turned upside down after the Civil War.

However, not all white southerners who felt this way were ultimately as harmless as the beautiful Scarlett O'Hara from *Gone with the Wind*. There were many for whom the need for vengeance began to consume, fanning the flames of destruction into burning rage. Florence also had residents such as these who were willing to use fire to deliberately destroy as the ultimate expression of the intensity of their rage toward those whom they believed had harmed them first, harm that may have included all that had been burned that was dear to them during the Civil War. These arsonists were usually ex-Confederate soldiers or family members of ex-Confederate soldiers who had died during the Civil War. They would often form vigilante gangs to express their rage by burning and destroying the property of their enemies, pillaging, killing, lynching, raping, maiming and otherwise attempting to continue to bully and intimidate them. For these ex-Confederate soldiers and their family members, the Civil War was not over. Humiliating defeat was something that their pride could not continue to bear without the unshakeable belief that the South would rise again. Many sympathizers turned a blind eye in

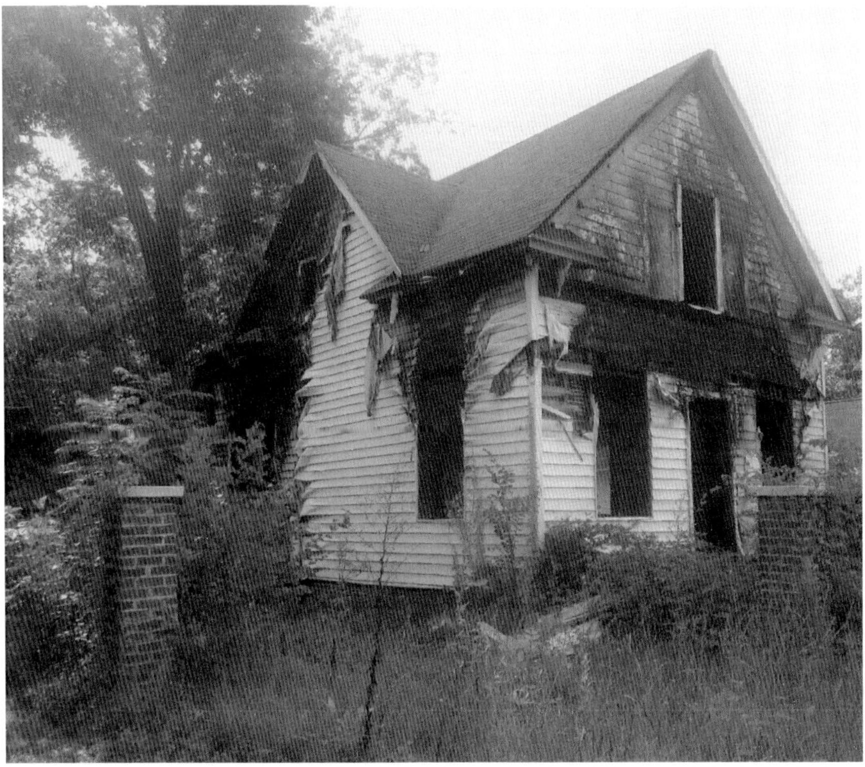

A mysterious house fire. *Author's collection.*

the wake of their vengeful destruction, resulting in these vigilantes rarely ever being held accountable for their crimes. As one historian wisely noted in a History Channel documentary, *Aftershock: Beyond the Civil War*, "The North won the Civil War, but the South won the War of Reconstruction."

Another key reason for destructive fires that was most problematic at the turn of the twentieth century was a physical one of nonexistent or insufficient building codes that would require builders to meet certain safety standards to help prevent or extinguish fires. The lack of enforceable safety standards became dangerous in American cities with a rapidly growing population during this time, such as Florence. The worst fire-related tragedies, notable when considering the amount of destruction and loss of life, were in the cities of Chicago, Peshtigo, Port Huron and New York. The most recognized fire in Florence was the Great Fire of 1899, which roared through the downtown business district, damaging and destroying many commercial buildings but killing no one. It was on the morning of December 18, one week before Christmas, when this conflagration began in the Central Hotel on Evans Street. This fire continued to burn out of control for at least twenty-four hours before it was contained, even jumping the block at two points to North Dargan Street to consume four commercial buildings, including the Florence Opera House, and to West Evans Street to consume the Bank of Florence, Florence City Hall and an adjacent fruit store. It remains uncertain as to who or what actually started this fire, which resulted in a total estimated financial loss of $150,000. Without knowing who or what, it is even more difficult if not impossible to clearly ascertain as to why the fire began.

The firefighters' water gave out at a crucial moment, which is why the fire was not quickly extinguished. This lack of water was strange considering that Florence was surrounded by swampland and having difficulty adequately draining these marsh lands, creating excess surface water throughout the city. There was even a large swampy pond of stagnant water on the corner of Evans and Irby Streets, just one block west of the intersection of Evans and Dargan Streets, that held enough water after a heavy rain that it was reported in the *Florence Morning News* to be "deep enough to swim a horse." This historic Florence District was listed in the National Register in 2008. The downtown district now includes a collection of thirty commercial buildings, with twenty-four contributing properties, all on Dargan and Evans Streets, two of the original seven streets of Florence.

Deliberate arson for financial gain was another key reason for destructive fires, particularly during the Great Depression. One magazine, the *New Outlook*, highlighted the growing "Burn Your Own Home" movement in

1933 that replaced the "Own Your Own Home" movement of the so-called Perpetual Prosperity era of the previous decade. The article noted that about three out of five arson cases were residential rather than commercial. "All over the country, residential fires are thirty to forty percent higher than they were for the previous year, and last year they were fifty percent higher than in the previous six years."

Was it for emotional, physical or financial reasons that an abandoned home less than a block away from the corner of Gaillard and Pine Streets began to suddenly burn out of control on February 9, 2017, or could there actually be a ghostly arsonist or arsonists involved, vengeful spirits who had finally had enough of this home that remained abandoned and neglected, an abandoned home believed to have been used as a haven to commit unspeakable crimes? Gaillard Street has developed an increasingly sordid reputation over the decades since Mr. Sulzbacher once lived in the neighborhood a century ago. Unfortunately, some areas of this street in Florence have become a den for criminals of all types, including those who

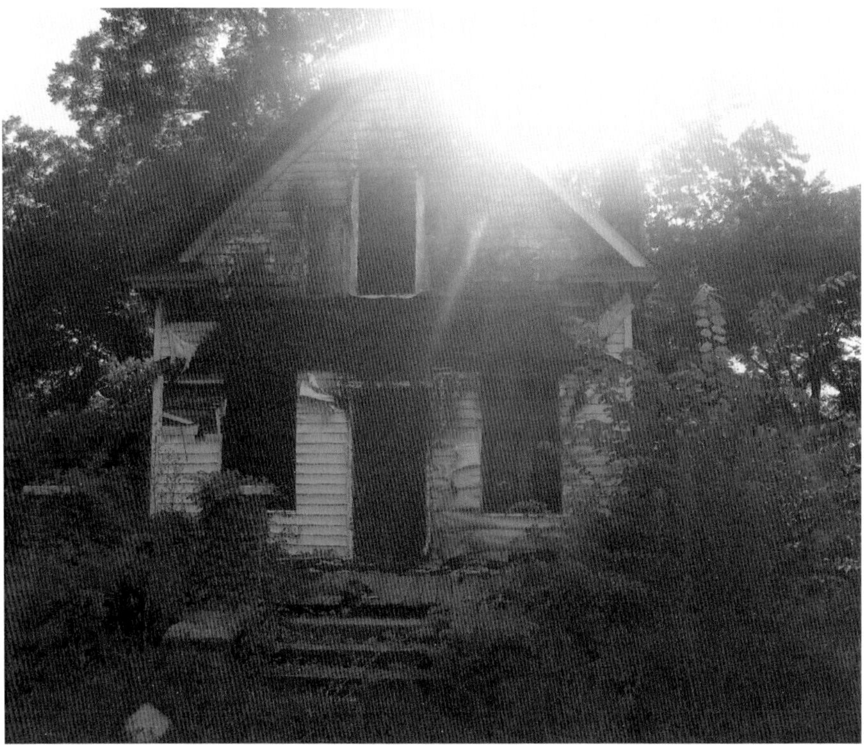

A burning of consequence. *Author's collection.*

are involved in drug and sex trafficking. In this underworld of desperation and depravity, even innocent children are often unable to escape without being abused, molested, traumatized and killed.

Some Florence residents in this neighborhood were not surprised but instead relieved when this abandoned home burned. A few believed that it was divine judgment from the spiritual realm for the crimes that they suspected had been committed there since this home was abandoned around the late 1990s, particularly crimes against children. Most of these neighbors were convinced that it was the lost souls of these once innocent children who became supernatural arsonists after several ghost sightings by more than one neighbor revealed what was described as the shimmering faces of crying children peering out from the front windows at night. Every time a neighbor would attempt to investigate, uncertain of what they might be seeing, there was no one there. The conclusion that these neighbors came to was that whatever crimes were committed there must have taken place before these phantasmal children began to draw supernatural attention to this now quite haunted home. Were these children the supernatural reason for this unexplained burning? Or could the ghostly arsonist who became the spark of this divine judgment be none other than Mr. Sulzbacher himself, watching over his neighborhood in the afterlife?

Stand on the large wooden platform at the front door of this home if you dare and look in closely, as the surreal faces of many different children may still appear from the shadows inside. If you look to the left, you may even see the shadow of an arrow pointing up appear on the exterior wall. Is this another clue from the great beyond that might reveal who the supernatural fire starter or fire starters are?

10
Lost

There is a vine-covered and boarded-up structure on the east side of Darlington Street that still looks like a boardinghouse today and is approximately a quarter of a mile from the historic Atlantic Coastline Railroad passenger depot. This boardinghouse has been acknowledged in Florence for being haunted by a couple dressed in turn-of-the-twentieth-century clothing. They can sometimes be seen in the early morning if you look up at a second-story window of this boardinghouse. There is a brief YouTube video about Florence ghosts that documents this haunting.

The Atlantic Coastline Railroad was a U.S. Class I railroad from 1900 to 1967. A Class I distinction was given to the largest companies in the industry. The Atlantic Coastline Railroad started as the Petersburg Railroad in 1830 and connected Petersburg, Virginia, to Weldon, North Carolina. Another connection was added from Petersburg to Richmond, Virginia, in 1836, becoming the Richmond and Petersburg Railroad. Weldon then connected with Wilmington, North Carolina, in 1840 and was renamed the Wilmington and Raleigh and then the Wilmington and Weldon Railroad in 1855. From Wilmington, Harllee's Wilmington and Manchester Railroad was chartered to officially connect to Florence, South Carolina, in 1853.

The Civil War destruction by Union soldiers of South Carolina railroads devastated the Wilmington and Manchester Railroad near its Manchester location. There was an attempt after the Civil War to revive the failing railroad, but to no avail. The Wilmington and Manchester declared bankruptcy in 1870. There was a brief attempt in 1871 to reorganize

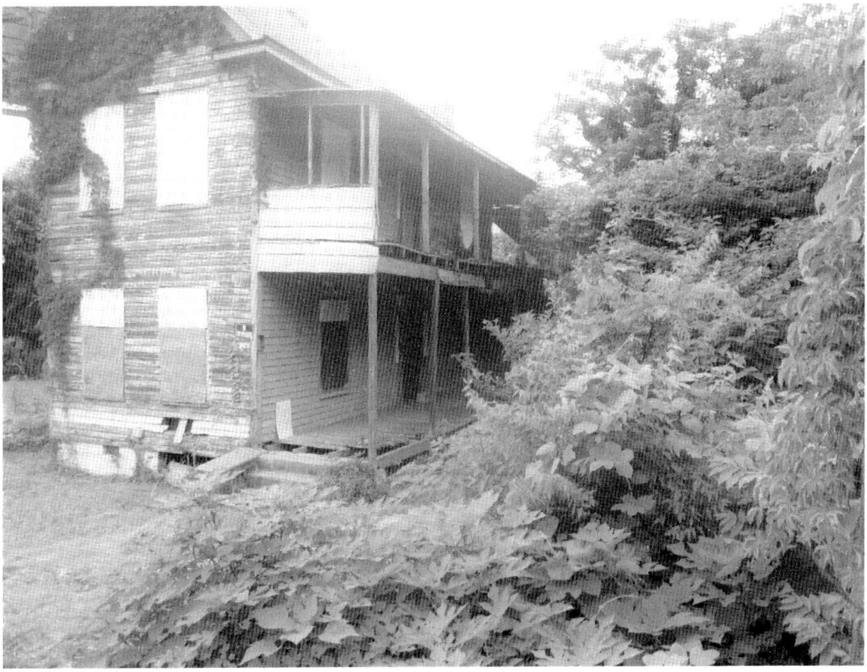

Still a boardinghouse for the lost. *Author's collection.*

the railroad as the Wilmington and Carolina Railroad and then as the Wilmington, Columbia and Augusta Railroad. An investor from Baltimore, Maryland, named William Walters soon gained control of these individual railroads and operated them as independent companies until the 1890s, when he began to consolidate them all into the Atlantic Coastline Railroad of South Carolina. Then, in 1900, another merger combined the Atlantic Coastline Railroads of North Carolina, South Carolina and Virginia into one much larger company with its headquarters in Virginia, due to the better regulatory climate there. Now there was only the Atlantic Coastline Railroad, which managed to encompass many of the formerly independent railroads from these three states.

In 1893, Florence still had the independent Cheraw and Darlington Railroad running north–south, with the merging Atlantic Coastline Railroad going east–west. There was an Atlantic Coastline Railroad warehouse located on Front Street. The Atlantic Coastline Railroad made a historic trip in 1894 when it connected Washington, D.C., to Jacksonville, Florida, with the fastest part of the trip between Ashley Junction and Florence in South

Carolina, traveling at an average speed of 58.3 miles per hour. By 1903, the enlarged Atlantic Coastline Railroad had encompassed the Cheraw and Darlington Railroad and constructed line car and repair shops, a coal elevator and a passenger depot and dining room on Florence's Front Street.

By 1908, there was a boardinghouse located on the eastern end of Darlington Street. It would be this same boardinghouse that developed a reputation for being haunted. The building changed the nature of its business several times during the mid-twentieth century, operating as a grocery store, a hardware store and a bicycle shop before it finally became abandoned toward the end of the 1900s. Perhaps it was the sudden silence of abandonment behind the walls of what was first a boardinghouse that provoked these two ghosts to begin to appear.

The most common ghost sighting at this location is that of an anxious couple. The man is older than the woman and dressed in overalls with a long-sleeved shirt underneath. He is standing over a woman who is dressed in a long-sleeved dress with many little buttons and a high collar. She is kneeling and frantically searching for something lost on the floor. What did she lose? An important piece of jewelry, such as a wedding ring? An important piece of paper, such as a receipt? Was this couple married? Why were they staying at this boardinghouse?

In 1910, the Atlantic Coastline Railroad's new train depot was completed on Day Street, just south of Front Street and less than a mile from the boardinghouse on Darlington Street. By 1912, the Atlantic Coastline Railroad had added freight sheds, a pumping station and a YMCA building in Florence, all in the Front Street area. In 1912, the Atlantic Coastline Railroad also had a competitor for the first time in Florence, the Seaboard Airline Railroad, which built a passenger depot on East Darlington Street, making it even closer to this particular boardinghouse.

First advertised as the "Route of Courteous Service," the Seaboard Airline Railroad focused on catering to passengers who were traveling south to Florida; its citrus-colored train designs and sunny advertisements promised visions of a tropical paradise when these passengers arrived. If you're slightly confused as to why a railroad would include the word *sea* and especially the word *airline* in its name, then you would not be alone. There were many investors who took an interest during the late 1920s when they thought that it was an aviation-related company, only to lose interest when they discovered that it was a railroad. Before the time of air travel, the term *airline* was used by railroads like the Seaboard to suggest that their tracks made it possible to travel the shortest distance between two destinations.

By 1918, the Seaboard Airline Railroad had added a freight warehouse in Florence and was advertising itself as "The Progressive Railroad of the South." The Atlantic Coastline Railroad was still holding steady but had not expanded with the construction of any new buildings since 1912. The boardinghouse situated between the passenger depots of these two railroads was still there on East Darlington Street in 1918. There were north–south Atlantic Coastline Railroad tracks that went right by the house.

Although it remains unclear what the woman in this ghostly couple may have lost, what does seem clear is that this couple had been staying at this boardinghouse because of the railroads—either as passengers or possibly because the man worked for one of the nearby railroads.

In what could be described as a mutually profitable truce in their longstanding business competition with each other that had lasted for close to seventy years, these two Class I railroads merged together in 1967 to form the Seaboard Coastline Railroad. After several more mergers, the Seaboard Coastline Railroad became CSX Transportation in 1986. The CSX Corporation still operates out of Florence today from a division office. Amtrak train services also are still offered to and from Florence.

The 1910 Atlantic Coastline Railroad passenger depot still stands today, but it is no longer used as a train depot and is instead medical offices. After Amtrak used this train depot for many years, the CSX Corporation built a newer train station for Amtrak right next to the location of the depot on Day Street in 1996. The Seaboard Airline Railroad passenger depot no longer exists. There is a state historical marker on Hoffmeyer Road that recognizes the original location of the first train depot named Florence, which William Harllee built in 1852. From 1852 to the construction of the newest train station of Florence in 1996 a century and a half had passed.

Did William Harllee ever envision how large the railroad corporations would become, or did he always envision the railroads as being many independent companies? How would he have considered the many mergers and changing of hands of these powerful railroads? Would he have made the same business deals? We will never know for sure what Harllee might have thought. Like so many other southerners though, Harllee's politics led to his enterprise becoming one of "Sherman's Neckties." Once a well-respected, well-established, well-connected and well-to-do winner, Harllee found his entire world turned upside down after the Civil War. He had suddenly become the loser, and lose he did, with the burning of his Sunnyside plantation to the ground in 1873 as the ultimate symbol of his defeat—just twenty-one years after one of the key

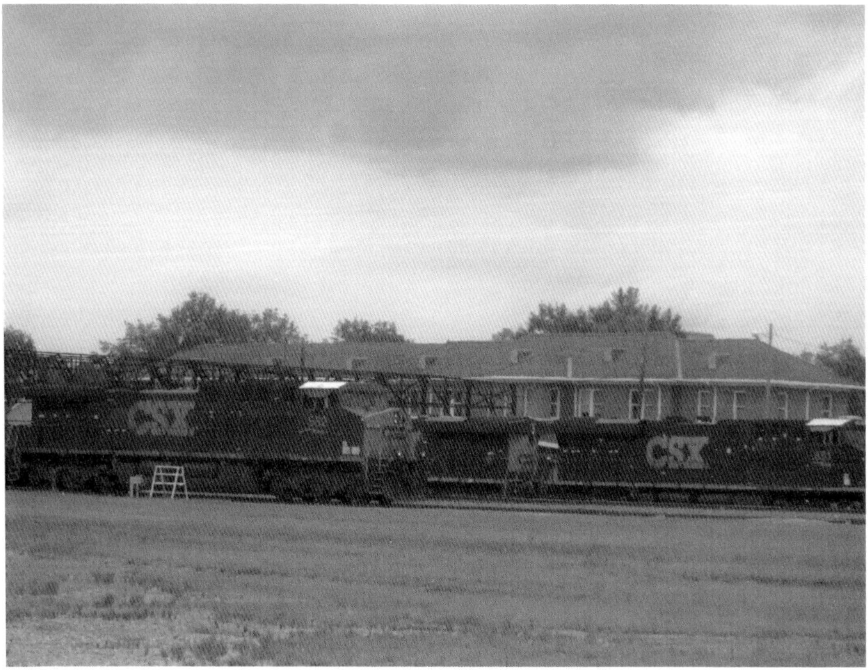

CSX rail yard nearby to boardinghouse and historic Atlantic Coastline Railroad depot. *Author's collection.*

moments in his life that had surely been one of his greatest triumphs. In 1873, Harllee was forced to leave his own city due to increasing financial ruin, the city named after his own daughter, Florence. William Harllee would never return to live in Florence again.

The birth era of Florence seemed to pass on with William Harllee in 1897, for in just three years, the transformative turning of the twentieth century would come. The roughhewn train depot named Florence became the state-of-the-art architectural design of Joseph Florence Leitner in 1910, when the Florence train depot moved on to its next destination. Sometimes what is lost is not something material, even in a material world; sometimes what is lost in the passing of time is an era gone by—requiring change, sometimes dramatic change, for those who are willing to transform into a new tomorrow.

11
When the Piano Plays

The Lawson-Chase House on Spruce Street is unoccupied and seemingly very lonely. It had once been a family home and was then open to the public, where countless numbers of people were able to be inspired by its unique blend of magic over the years. Some people still visit this location, even after it has been closed, and desire to go inside, whether from nostalgia as locals or from ignorance as tourists who have still not realized yet that the Florence Museum has officially moved to its new location. There is a timeless and magical mystique that does seem to surround this home and only becomes more powerful when the piano plays, a haunting melody of bittersweet notes that has been heard coming from inside this home and former museum. While standing at the front entrance, more than a few visitors were quite taken by surprise when they realized that this home was no longer occupied or the location of the Florence Museum. Who is this ghostly piano player or spiritual DJ of a timeless tune who still seeks to connect and bring life to this now empty and tomb-like place?

It was William Harllee who was the founder of the Magic City of Florence in 1852, and he did so with the rugged flair of a rough-hewn train depot at the crossing of three railroads. His influence and legacy laid the foundation for Florence to grow and flourish even during the Civil War era, a tumultuous and challenging time in American history that could have caused the city's destruction instead of its ultimate prosperity. Wise and shrewd leadership after the Civil War made it possible for Florence to rejoin

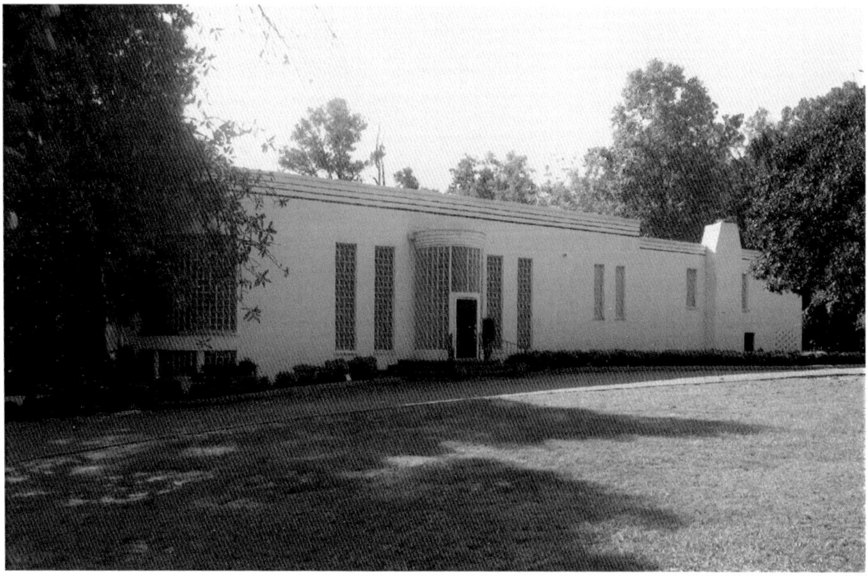

The Lawton-Chase House, also the old Florence Museum. *Author's collection.*

the Union without as much turmoil and upheaval that many southern cities experienced during the Reconstruction period.

Jerome Chase became the first mayor of the newly chartered Florence in 1871 and has been called the father of Florence. Chase came to Florence with his wife, Harriet Gordon McLeod, in 1866. They had three sons—Jerome Jr. (May 13, 1852—July 1, 1932), Lawson (March 20, 1868—March 22, 1910) and Sanborn (October 5, 1870–August 2, 1926)—and one daughter, Clara (March 20, 1877–October 4, 1957). Jerome Chase was born on July 28, 1838, and worked on a railroad during the Civil War. He then briefly worked as a telephone operator before moving to Florence. Soon after moving to Florence, Chase became coeditor of the first Florence weekly newspaper, the *Gazette.* He and a business partner bought the paper in 1868 and renamed it the *Pioneer.* Chase's political interests led to him becoming successful in the real estate and insurance business by the early 1890s. His firm was then called Jerome Chase & Sons. The population of Florence tripled from 1900 to 1920, and real estate, along with the insurance business, kept booming as a result. Jerome Chase died in 1916, the same year as his wife, Harriet, and he left his real estate and insurance firm to his sons. Florence has streets that honor this branch of the Chase family over a century later: Chase Street,

Lawson Street and Sanborn Street were all added to the city between 1913 and 1918. Chase Street is between Lawson Street and Sanborn Street, with Lawson Street to the left and Sanborn Street to the right.

Sanborn Chase married Kloo Glenn of Tampa, Florida, in 1913. They had one son, Sanborn Jr. Sanborn Sr. continued his father Jerome's wealthy and prosperous legacy in the real estate and insurance business. In 1918, Sanborn Chase Sr.'s net financial worth was estimated to be $2.3 million (adjusting for inflation today, approximately a century later, equal to about $37 million). The earliest version of Monopoly was called the Landlord's Game, first patented by Elizabeth Magie in 1904. Sanborn may have even been like the iconic Mr. Monopoly in real life before the board game was immortalized by Parker Brothers in 1935, wheeling and dealing properties throughout the city in the same fashion of the time for men of financial wealth, complete with a black top hat, suit, gloves and cane. Sanborn was on the board of directors of the Pee Dee Trust Company and the Peoples Savings Bank and Trust. He and Kloo were married for thirteen years until his death on August 2, 1926.

Could Kloo Chase be the mysterious piano player from beyond the grave who still haunts the Lawton-Chase House today? At least one nostalgic Magic City resident who visited this location and knew the history of this home thought so. He was convinced that Kloo shared so many fond memories with her second husband, Joseph Lawton, in their home together that she returns to sentimentally remember these romantic moments by playing one of their favorite songs.

Sanborn's wife, Kloo, continued the family business after her husband's passing and waited for over a decade before remarrying. One of the properties that she owned after Sanborn's death became the Pee Dee Community Center, known locally as Happy Hours. Happy Hours was the grand vision of a man named Keith Lockwood. In 1925, he wanted to develop a lavish resort to bring the exuberant fun of the Roaring Twenties to the Pee Dee region, particularly for the wealthy elite. This posh resort included a restaurant, a bowling alley, a beauty shop, a convention center, a dance hall, a Ferris wheel and a large swimming pool. The opening of Happy Hours was quite the eagerly anticipated social event for many Florentines. Happy Hours did not disappoint with its grand opening on December 31, 1926, even though the facility was not completely finished. Unfortunately, Sanborn was not physically able to be there for this grand opening, having passed on approximately five months prior. It is uncertain whether Kloo attended the New Year's Eve dance at Happy Hours without him.

This New Year's Eve dance at Happy Hours was such a popular success that many dazzling social events quickly followed, including a Valentine's Day masquerade dance. Perhaps one of this dance's most memorable attractions was a large conch shell made of glass that decorated the musicians' stage in the dance hall, with two hundred reflecting lights of various colors that flashed intermittently in waves through the shell, further exciting the romantic imagination of the relatively carefree Roaring Twenties for many. It is possible that this shell may have even been an early technical example of the disco balls that adorned so many dance clubs in the 1970s, both symbolic of decades in American history that were characterized by youthful idealism, the quest for virtually unlimited social freedom without restriction and what some might also characterize as increasingly reckless fun without consequence. So it was with Happy Hours, when a tragic accident approximately seven months after its grand opening in July 1927 resulted in the good times abruptly coming to an end after a man broke his neck and later died by diving into the shallow end of the swimming pool. It would be easy to conclude that this man must have been intoxicated to have behaved so foolishly, but such a conclusion has never been definitively confirmed. It is difficult to understand why the personal tragedy of one man, W.W. Register, would cause Happy Hours to go from being so popular to temporarily shut down approximately one year later in March 1928. Reportedly, Lockwood's creditors, to whom he was deeply in debt, became nervous after this tragic accident occurred and soon demanded payment. Lockwood was unable to pay back his debts and had to file for bankruptcy.

It was in February 1928 that Kloo Chase, who held the mortgage on the Happy Hours property, began foreclosure proceedings. Kloo briefly reopened Happy Hours for approximately one more year with her brother Clyde Glenn in charge of the daily operations of the resort. Happy Hours permanently closed in the summer of 1929, an ironic foreshadowing of what would soon take place with the stock market crash on October 29, 1929. The Great Depression immediately followed like some fearsome specter of judgment against the overly optimistic recklessness and wild extravagance of the 1920s—where debt often far exceeded the real money to pay those debts off for far too many. Kloo Chase sold the former Happy Hours property in March 1930 and was one of a relative few who was able to continue to prosper and grow despite the most terrible economic downturn in the history of the United States. Kloo had married Joseph Lawton by 1939, approximately thirteen years after her first husband's death. Lawton was a builder by trade, quite a complementary profession to Kloo's real estate business.

Could it be Joseph Lawton rather than Kloo who still returns to haunt the Lawton-Chase House in an attempt to relive the joyful romance that he had once shared with her? At least one other Magic City resident who was familiar with the history of this house and the Chase family was convinced that it must be Joseph instead of Kloo because Kloo would be much too serious and practical of a personality to be involved in such a sentimental gesture after death. However, the individual agreed with what most Magic City residents who are familiar with this haunting believe, that of the three residents—Kloo, Joseph and Kloo's son, Sanborn Jr.—who were most likely to be haunting the home today, Sanborn Jr. was the most likely spirit, as he was the most sentimentally attached to this location.

Sanborn Chase Jr. was born on January 5, 1919. He was only seven years old when his father died and approximately twenty years old when his mother remarried. How surreal it must have been at times for Sanborn Jr. to grow up as a wealthy teenager during the Great Depression and lonely as an only child without a father. However, by the time his mother remarried, Sanborn Jr. was able to welcome and embrace Joseph Lawton enough into his family to design their new home on Spruce Street in Florence to be ready to move in by 1939. Sanborn Jr. was a college student at the time and studying engineering. His architectural design was unique and influenced by Moderne architecture in France. The new Lawton-Chase home on Spruce Street was reported to have become the talk of the town after its completion.

The Lawton-Chase House on Spruce Street was the Florence Museum for sixty years, from 1953 to 2013. This unique home was recognized by a South Carolina historical marker in 2011. The trustees and supporters of the Florence Museum continued to promote the arts, culture, science and history through a variety of educational programs, lectures and musical performances—including the piano—and they created many inspiring and magical moments for Florentines and others to appreciate and enjoy during the decades that the museum was there. This enduring endeavor of the Florence Museum at this location seems to be quite a fitting legacy for the man who first designed his home with all of the artistic and creative flair and inspired promise of his youthful exuberance and spirited passion. Maintenance issues and the need for more space to expand were reported to be the main reasons why the Florence Museum moved to its new location to on East Cheves Street as the Florence County Museum.

A few seemingly more practical-minded Florentines were convinced that the haunting of this location is not connected to the time when it was the home of the Lawton-Chase family but to when it became the Florence Museum. These Florentines believe that the nostalgic spirit has to be one of the piano players who performed at the Florence Museum, although they are uncertain of which piano player it might be. They supported their belief by emphasizing the timing of when this location first began to be rumored to be haunted—after the museum was closed. If it was a member of the Lawton-Chase family haunting this location, then the haunting would have begun before the home became the Florence Museum.

Sanborn Jr. was supportive of the Florence Little Theatre; he even built a stage for performances in the backyard of his new home on Spruce Street when the Florence Little Theatre was temporarily without a home. In the summertime, Sanborn Jr. directed a play performed there called *The Drunkard; or, The Fallen Saved*. This drama was a spoof of an old Victorian melodrama that includes the characters of a good brother and a bad brother. At the end of the play, the villainous brother is thrown into the swimming pool in the backyard on closing night. Sanborn Jr. enjoyed acting as well, and on March 1, 1951, the *Florence Morning News* reported he was acting in a comedy called *A Date with Judy*. Sanborn Jr. played a small role as a character who is described as a "near-ulcerated man who is tired of his profession" and is seeking some excitement in his life by visiting an old friend but gets even more drama than he expected.

In the 1940s, Sanborn Jr. married Madge DeFosset, and they had a daughter and a son named Sandra and Sanborn (III). In 1946, they founded the Vulcraft Corporation together, an industrial steel fabrication facility that still has a division located in Florence today. In 1953, a strike was reported, but it is uncertain as to exactly why the workers chose to strike or how many of the 150 workers actually went on strike during this time. Vulcraft's public relations director Alfred Lawton indicated that management had anticipated the workers striking for about six months. One possible outcome of the strikes, though, was that in 1954, Vulcraft chose to exclusively manufacture long and short span joists. The Vulcraft Corporation became Nucor Corporation and grew to expand throughout the United States. The business has gone international, with two new Canadian divisions added in 2017.

Sanborn Chase Jr. passed away on July 20, 1961, at home after becoming very ill at the age of forty-two years old. Having been wealthy from birth and understandably no longer as motivated to acquire even more wealth, would Sanborn Jr. have been thrilled and proud of such a tremendously profitable and successful business expansion of a corporation that he helped found, or would his true heart have ultimately remained enthralled and motivated instead by the greater freedom of expression from the performing arts that he found in the creative life of the theater? Is that why most of the Magic City residents who are familiar with this haunted place on Spruce Street believe that it must be Sanborn Jr. who still attempts to bring life back to the home that he designed? It quite possibly does contain some of the most personally poignant and heartfelt moments of his life and they are so compelling that he must return from beyond the grave to continue to remember them. Whoever it may be, when the piano plays its timeless tune here, the spirit of Florence, the City of Magic, must grow even stronger.

12

Foster Care and a Scowling Stare

It is uncertain what might have been located on one particular plat of land on South Dargan Street before there was a mansion built there in 1925. It is also uncertain why this mansion was built as a private residence in the middle of what was a commercial district or who the original owners were and how long they actually lived there. One possible clue is that the first Florence Public Library was built the same year less than a mile away in what appears to be a similar architectural design—Neoclassical Revival with Beaux Arts influences. They probably were designed by the same Florence architectural firm, Wilkins and Hopkins. Perhaps the original owner of this mansion was a patron of the arts in Florence during the 1920s. The city became increasingly concerned about the welfare of its residents, along with the rest of the United States, during the era of charity in the 1890s–1910s—known as the Progressive Reform era—when enough Americans became morally convicted by the social and financial inequality of their society to endeavor to do good works to improve the conditions of the less fortunate. This charitable response by social reformers was in reaction to the increasingly stark contrast between the lifestyles of the very rich and the very poor created by the unbridled greed of unregulated capitalism.

Those who approach this vacant mansion on South Dargan Street today may feel a sense of ominous foreboding, as if some virtually hidden force is attempting to discourage anyone from entering. Some Florentines have even reported seeing a large spirit orb near a second-floor bedroom

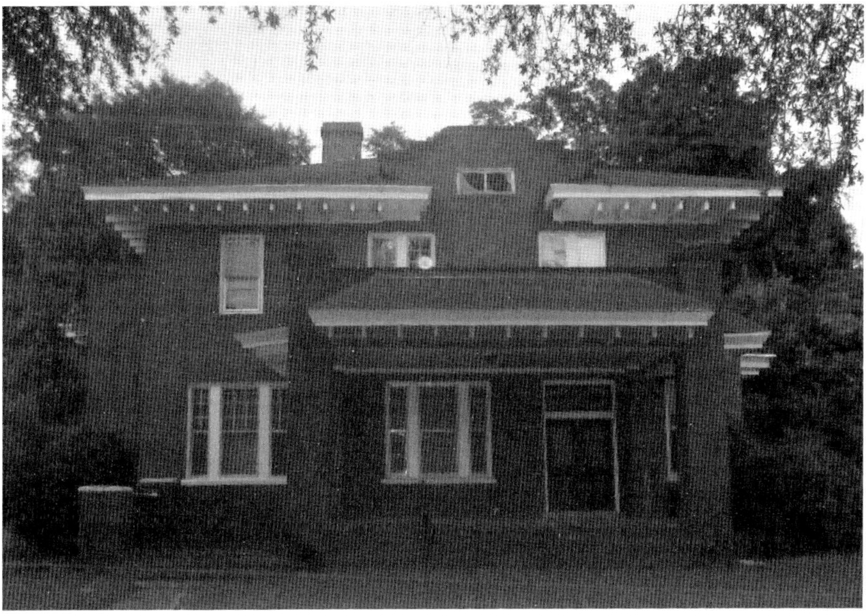

Former foster care home with spirit orb near front second-floor bedroom window. *Author's collection.*

window. Closer examination may reveal the scowling face of a stout woman in her fifties with graying hair, dressed in a black shroud, who has been sighted by more than one extraordinary observer. This threatening ghost is described as having long hair that is pulled up into two buns on either side of her face, and she is menacingly holding a cane while staring out of this bedroom window. Why is she trying to discourage people from entering this home? What is she guarding so covetously, even after death? This property or something much more damning, like sinister secrets of the abominable abuse and neglect of children that was done in the name of discipline? What is certain is that by the 1970s, this mansion had begun to be used as a group home for foster children by more than one agency and continued to be used for foster care services until recently, when this property became vacant and was then listed for sale in 2017.

Prior to the Progressive movement, children were often placed in orphanages simply because their parents were too poor to care for them. By 1920, forty out of the forty-eight states of America offered some kind of financial aid to poor families. Sadly, South Carolina was not one of these forty states. Instead, in 1909, Florence proudly boasted of being the location of the first state institution of its kind in the Pee Dee, the Industrial School for Boys. This school offered placement for children who were no longer able to remain in their own homes. The days at this school were filled with hard labor, and conditions there were typical of institutional living for foster children, with abuse, neglect and brutal discipline part of their routine.

The terrible conditions for children in orphanages was one great concern of the Progressive era. Orphanages were institutionalized and regimented and no longer deemed appropriate to foster the positive growth and development of children. Proper supervision of large numbers of children at a time was almost always lacking, making it commonplace for children to be abused in these institutions, either by the adults or by other children. Many orphanages attempted to reform themselves in response to the Progressive criticisms. However, most Progressives were not convinced that placing children in orphanages was better than placing them in foster homes, and they continued to advocate for foster homes as the better alternative. It soon became apparent, though, that foster homes were not the ideal solution for at-risk children because they were still being abused and neglected in foster homes.

Not really orphanages and not really foster homes, children's group homes began to become more and more common as another alternative placement for children who could no longer remain with their parents. Group homes offered a more home-like rather than institutional setting, with the maximum number of children being placed in one home being regulated to about fifteen at a time. Group homes did not provide the solution though either to the continued widespread abuse and neglect of disadvantaged children in the foster care system.

Dargan Street was one of the original seven streets, recorded there as early as 1858, long before the city was officially incorporated in 1890. Over time, Dargan Street became a blended street of both commercial and residential properties, with the northern section part of the first commercial business district in Florence. The southern part of Dargan Street developed later and, at first, was more commercial than residential. City maps note that by 1898, the southern part of Dargan Street had become fully developed.

Gunshots were fired on the front lawn of this haunted mansion on South Dargan Street one night around 9:00 p.m. on June 8, 2010, in a shooting incident that involved five teenagers. A teenage boy was shot in the side, and a girl was shot in the face. Three boys were arrested for this shooting, with one of the boys turning himself in. Why were these teenagers shot at this location? Were they all living here? Were all of the teenagers involved foster children?

So many questions still remain as to what might have taken place behind the closed doors of this particular foster home and how many children lived there over the decades. Who were the staff members who supervised these children? Was it only a foster home, or were academic education services ever offered there to any of these foster children as well? Perhaps walking around to the back or inside this seemingly vacant mansion might help answer some of these questions.

A nearby neighbor claimed to have seen another ghostly image through an upstairs window. This apparition appears to be of a different woman, much younger and thinner, who is wearing a long dress and has her hair pulled up into a bun at the nape of her neck. She is sitting in a chair at a desk, and her eyes are deeply shadowed and hollowed with grief and sorrow. However, this may not be a different woman after all. This ghost sighting might reveal instead a greater paranormal insight as to why the scowling ghost seen at the front of this spooky mansion became the way that she did as she grew older. Was there some great tragedy such as the death or loss of a beloved foster child in her care when she was much younger that caused her

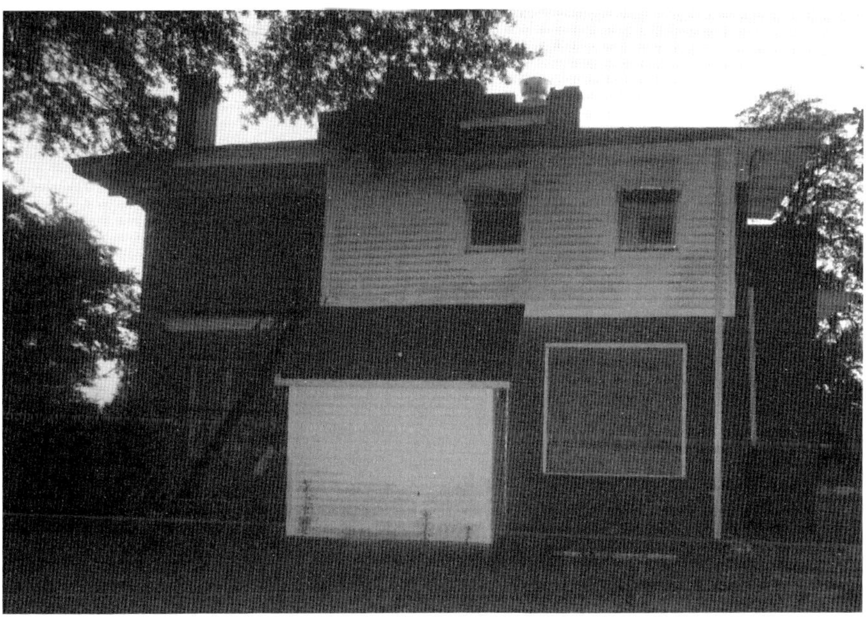

Former foster care home, back view. *Author's collection.*

heart to become so filled with disillusionment and then cloaked by a great shroud of mean-spirited bitterness?

Even so, if you still dare to walk inside, two aspects of this haunted mansion might draw your psychic intuition most profoundly. In the bedroom where the woman with a cane has been seen, there may still be a large wardrobe adjacent to the window that seems very oddly out of place. Next to the kitchen area, there is a long tunnel and an image on the wall at the beginning of this tunnel of a woman who looks similar to the woman with the cane. She is wearing glasses, her tongue is slightly protruding into the grimace of a smile and there is what appears to be a wooden clothespin on the top of her head. What could this image possibly mean? And who or what might be revealing any evil secrets, even now? If only the walls could talk.

13

What a Price to Pay

It has been rumored that a strange curse has fallen over the home and land of a former Florentine store owner, keeping would-be renters and buyers away, for it is a property that continues to remain abandoned today. Gloom and despair seem to permeate this place and the nearby railroad crossing at Price Road. According to local legend, it was the mysterious case of a missing bag from an Atlantic Coastline train on All Fool's Day that was the cause of this dreadful curse.

Florence was the largest rail hub in South Carolina in the 1940s, with fourteen passenger trains and forty-eight freight trains traveling north, south, east and west on a daily basis. During World War II, the Atlantic Coastline Railroad became an important part of the rapidly emerging military industry in the Southeast. The Atlantic Coastline Railroad passenger traffic increased 200 percent, and its freight traffic increased 150 percent, in part due to the ongoing threat by German submarines during this time to coastal shipping.

The Atlantic Coastline Railroad was never attacked by the Germans. However, the railroad was attacked by the general public, its passengers and even occasionally by its own staff, who were involved in damage to its trains and loss of property over the decades. Loss of property was a very serious matter to the railroads, particularly passenger baggage and belongings. No railroad wanted to develop a reputation for its passengers or their belongings being unsafe in any way aboard its trains or at its stations. Such a reputation could be financially devastating even more than the loss of property itself

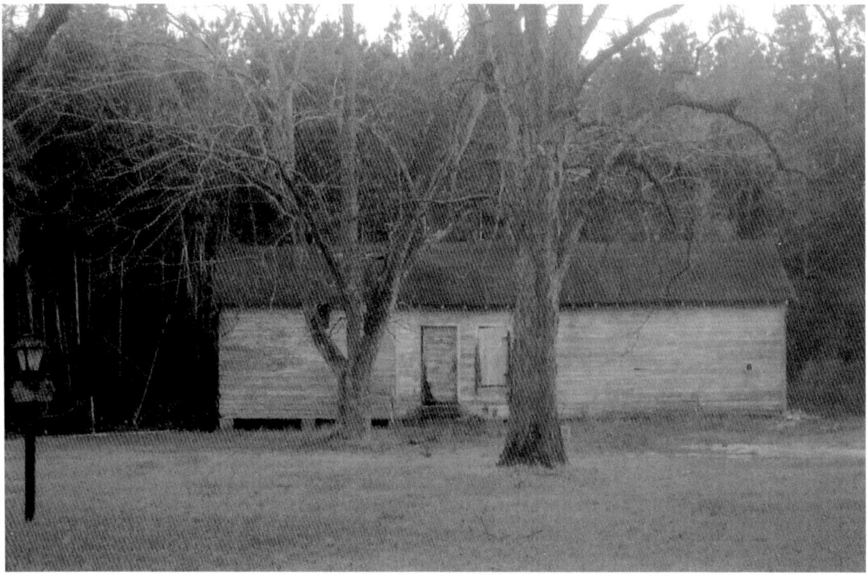

A view of the old general store from the railroad track. *Author's collection.*

to any railroad in such a highly competitive business. There were no great train robberies of the Atlantic Coastline Railroad. This railroad, along with many of its competitors, took great care to ensure that security was tight, and its operations were well monitored at all times. The railroads continue to have their own police officers who are responsible for every aspect of railroad security, including patrolling, monitoring and investigating any reports of trespassing, destruction of property, arson, theft and even assaults and murders that might take place on railroad property. Fewer than twenty-five reports of lost property were noted during the 1940s for the Atlantic Coastline Railroad.

J.A. Dorsey was the captain of police for the Atlantic Coastline Railroad at the Florence station during the 1940s. There were three incidents of lost property directly involving the Florence station that Captain Dorsey was never able to satisfactorily resolve. One incident occurred during World War II when the barracks bag of Claude Ebel was lost while he was traveling from Fort Myers, Florida, to Las Vegas, Nevada, in 1943 during military leave over the Christmas holidays. Unfortunately, his bag was never recovered. A second incident occurred the day after Valentine's Day in 1947 when D.R. Taylor reported that his gray suitcase and topcoat had gone missing while he was traveling to Jacksonville, Florida. Two coach cars were cut out of the main passenger train that Taylor had been traveling on in Florence, adding to the confusion. These lost items were never recovered either. The third incident was much more mysterious than the first two, involving a possible ghost of a passenger with a doppelganger bag who was never identified and some "deadheads."

It was on All Fool's Day, April 1, 1949, when this mysterious case of a lost bag occurred on the Atlantic Coastline Railroad train en route to Jacksonville, Florida, that day. A brown Gladstone bag was lost by a man named John Aille who reportedly did not realize that his bag was missing until the train arrived in Charleston, after it had passed through Florence. He later changed his account and stated he was not certain when his bag had gone missing. However, it was noted by car attendant T.J. Scott that Aille had stated that he had been up most of the night smoking due to pain from a back injury and should have realized when his bag had gone missing, especially since he was observed out on the platform of the car by Scott at every stop that the train had made.

There is a local Florence legend that an old black man found a lost bag around the same time in the evening hours, though no one knows the exact day in 1949 for sure, and that this bag contained a large amount of money, though no one knows for sure the exact amount. The bag was found right near an Atlantic Coastline train track that intersects with Price Road in Florence, an intersection close enough to any train going by that it could have even been thrown out of a train to be picked up later. Most Atlantic Coastline Railroad employees, particularly local workers in Florence, were familiar with all of the tracks and any convenient and necessary hiding places, as the case may be.

There were very few other passengers on the train with Aille who might have been able to take his bag on April 1, other than about five other passengers and two deadheads, railroad workers or relatives of railroad workers who therefore had the perk of riding the train on a free pass. Curiously, there was a passenger included in the incident report who was never identified. Aille insisted this unknown passenger was the man who must have mistakenly taken his bag. Aille described this man as an unemployed railroad worker about five foot seven or five foot eight with a slim build between thirty-five and forty years old. Aille believed that this unidentified person had mistakenly taken his bag because he also had a similar-looking brown bag. However, a thorough check of all of the remaining luggage on the train did not produce another brown bag that would explain this mistaken exchange. Even more curious,

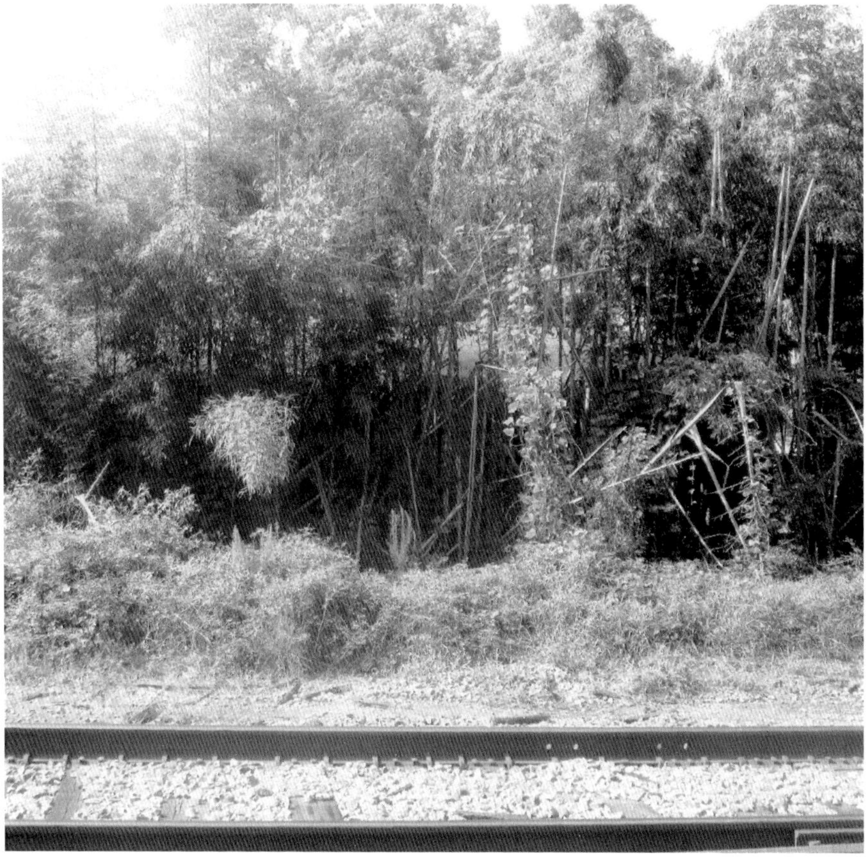

A crossing of regret. *Author's collection.*

when questioned, Scott, the car attendant, could not provide a physical description of this passenger or recall what seat he had occupied, even though he had a conversation with him about working on the railroad. Scott also could not recall what railroad that he had said that he worked for or where he was from. Scott did state that he thought that the mystery man might have worked in the non-operating department because he kept talking about "the changes which were to be made in the near future."

The two deadheads were a nineteen-year-old student named Henry Buist Jr., the son of a Seaboard Airline Railroad employee, and a fifty-nine-year-old railroad engineer for the Atlantic Coastline Railroad named S.E. Fleming. Strangely, Fleming, a resident of Florence, had been unreachable for an interview about this loss of property for several weeks before he was finally interviewed by Sergeant C.E. Sansbury at his home. Apparently, Fleming had been off duty due to poor health. The engineer stated that he had no recollection of Aille or a brown Gladstone bag. Buist was attending Yale University, and he was not interviewed at all because he was not expected to return home to Charleston until the summer.

Aille reported that his bag had contained only clothing and a few other personal items, so it would seem that this whole investigation was much ado over virtually nothing. However, Aille was extraordinarily distressed over the loss of his bag and continued to insinuate that the railroad employees in question had been deliberately negligent regarding its recovery. Is it possible that his bag contained something much more valuable than used clothing and a few personal items? If the local legend is true, then this Gladstone bag did in fact contain something very valuable after all—a substantial amount of money. Perhaps Aille had not been up all night due to back pain but to keep watch on his bag, which he still ended up losing anyway.

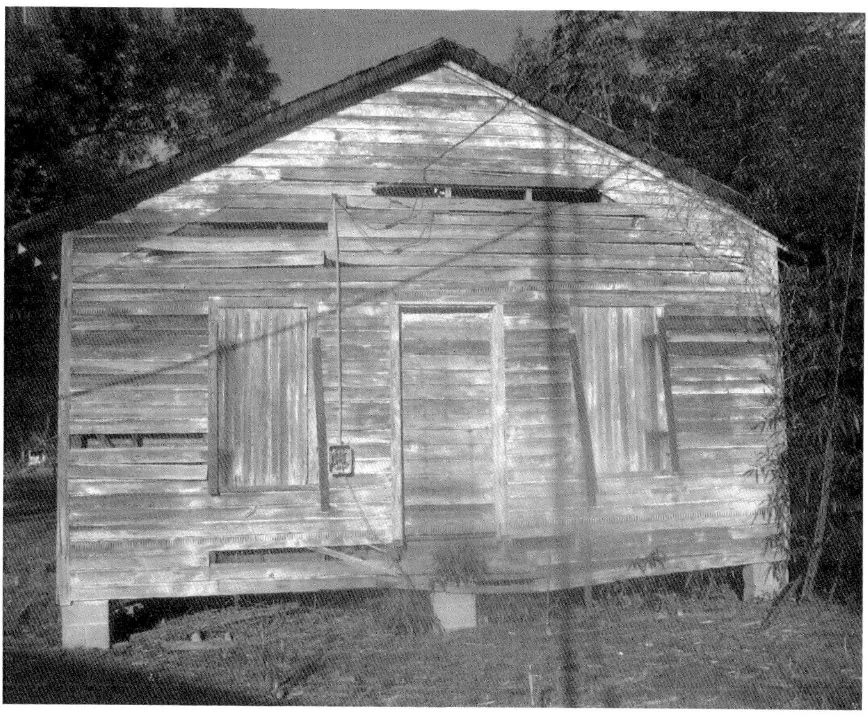

The old general store nearby to the railroad crossing at Price Road. *Author's collection.*

According to the rest of the legend, the seemingly lucky old man who had found this lost bag was in such a joyful state of shock over this sudden turn of fortune that his first move after finding the bag of money was to go into a nearby store, presumably to buy something. This man did not end up leaving the store with his bag of money, only a cigar and a Pepsi. Some say that the bag of money was taken from him by force, and some say that he turned the bag of money in to the store owner as a good deed to help return it to its rightful owner and the store owner gave him a cigar and a Pepsi in return for his reward. However, the bag was never returned to its rightful owner.

The supernatural twist to this local Florence legend speaks to the haunting of this area. The air becomes heavy at dusk, so heavy with regret that a misty cloud might surround you around the railroad crossing at Price Road. It is believed that this misty cloud is a phantasmal manifestation of a lost soul. Most Florentines are convinced that it is most likely the cursed soul of the store owner who now haunts this area. Is it the former store owner? Or the old man who found this lost bag? Could it be a deadhead? A former Atlantic Coastline Railroad employee? Or even John Aille? Whoever it may be, it certainly was a fool's price to pay on this day.

14
Shock and Sorrow

Diseases that can kill are a painful, even heartbreaking reminder of the frailty of physical humanity; life can be here in the body and then gone in an instant to never return. Sometimes these diseases can be even more painfully prolonged so that all who are close to this person must bear witness to the pain and suffering of the sickly and their physical degradation. Perhaps the most painful experience of all is to watch this pain and suffering in your own child and be left feeling helpless to stop this disease. Some Florentines believe one such family who did suffer this awful fate is caught by time in shock and sorrow and still haunts their abandoned and decaying home on East Pine Street. In 1928, the mortality rate per 1,000 infants born was almost 1 in 100 at 96.5 in the state of South Carolina. Only one state had a higher infant mortality rate at this time—Arizona—at 141.5 infant deaths per 1,000 infants born. The good news was that by 1946, the mortality rate in South Carolina per 1,000 infants born had been drastically reduced to 32.3. However, even at this significantly lower rate, South Carolina had the highest infant death rate in the entire nation; West Virginia had the second-highest rate at 31.5. Both states were included in the South Atlantic region—along with Delaware, Maryland, Virginia, North Carolina, Georgia, Florida and the District of Columbia—which had the highest infant mortality rate when measured overall of 27.5.

Why did South Carolina have the highest infant mortality rate in the United States in 1946? There were many factors that apparently contributed to this morbid outcome, such as the state still being predominantly rural and poor overall, with limited access to healthcare, improved sanitation and better nutrition outside of Charleston, Columbia and Florence. Mothers who were already in poor health also had babies who became more prone to sickness and death. In Florence in 1946, there were two hospitals that were noted for offering quality medical care. However, Florence still struggled significantly with pediatric diseases like tuberculosis, with a 10 percent infant mortality rate noted for all births to this disease in 1946.

McLeod Infirmary was within walking distance of this distressed family's home on East Pine Street in 1946. Did these parents bring their sick baby back and forth to this infirmary, or did medical staff come to their home? For doctors and all medical professionals, what a rollercoaster ride it must be of success or failure in circumstances like these to protect and defend themselves and others against the enemies of disease and death.

McLeod Infirmary was the first hospital in Florence and was founded by Frank Hilton McLeod in 1906. Frank was born in North Carolina and graduated from the University of Tennessee Medical School. Dr.

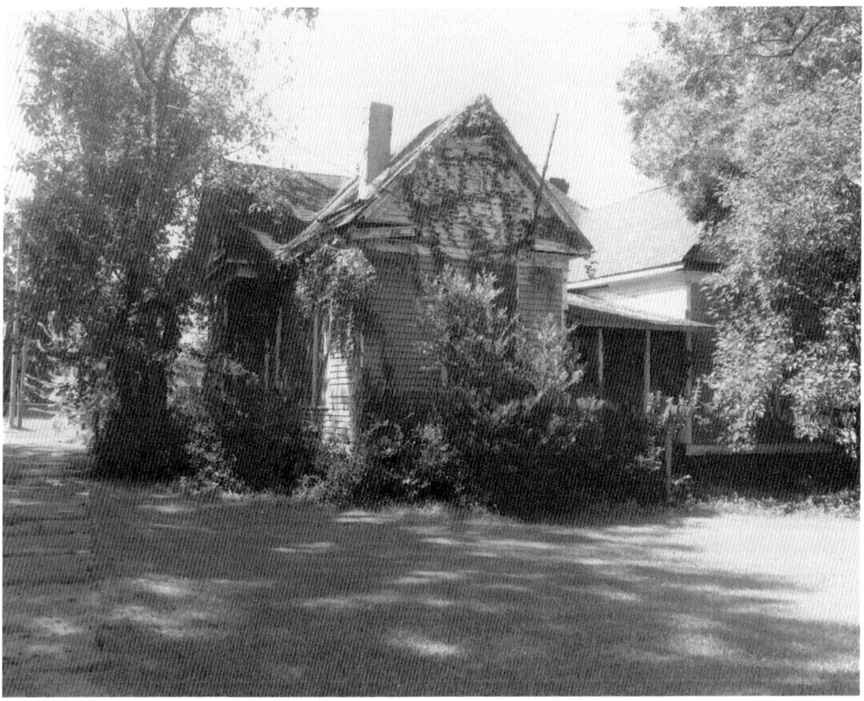

Going back home from McLeod Infirmary. *Author's collection.*

McLeod moved to Florence and began his medical practice there in 1899. Dr. McLeod was inspired to collaborate with other Florence doctors and open this hospital after a little boy named Rufus Barringer fell from a second-story window of the Central Hotel, right nearby to his medical office on Evans Street. There was nowhere nearby to treat the little boy's severe injuries, including a crushed skull. Dr. McLeod and other doctors attempted to do what they could, but they could not stop him from dying. Dr. McLeod became the foremost physician in the Pee Dee region and fulfilled his vision to have a hospital that would make it possible to meet all of the medical needs of the Florence community. The McCleod family had a history in Florence that began with Martha Jane May McLeod, daughter of Napoleon and Mary Jane Williams McLeod, who married William Norris in 1857.

A second hospital in Florence was founded in 1923 by Dr. John Smyser and was named Saunders Memorial Hospital in memory of his father-in-law. Across the street, the Bruce Hospital was founded in 1944 by Dr. John Bruce. Saunders Memorial Hospital was later sold to two brothers named Frank and Lamar Lee in 1949. In 1971, Saunders Memorial Hospital became the Florence General Hospital. Florence General Hospital and the Bruce Hospital joined together in 1989 and became what is now called the Carolinas Hospital System. Today, the first hospital in Florence is the McLeod Regional Medical Center.

In the 1940s, the McLeod Infirmary and Saunders Memorial Hospital were well recognized for providing medical care to Florentines in need. As it did in other American cities and towns, World War II came to overshadow most of the decade. Florence added a military base at the airport that served as a major training location during World War II. After the war, most veterans were eager to return to their families or start new ones. Unfortunately, one disease that many soldiers contracted while fighting in World War II was tuberculosis. One veteran was described in Mark D. Van Ells's book *To Hear Thunder Again: America's World War II Veterans Come Home* as being socially stigmatized for the first time after being diagnosed with this disease when he returned home. Prior to that time, tuberculosis was a disease that "poor families got." Another disease that had reached an all-time low but then resurged again during World War II was diphtheria. Although many efforts were made to prevent the spread of these two highly contagious diseases, when veterans returned home, such efforts were not completely successful. Many do not consider that the aftermath of war can lead to the dramatic rise in the devastation, destruction and death that communicable diseases like these can cause, despite the herculean efforts of the medical and science professions to combat them. Infants born in the years that immediately followed World War II were the most susceptible to four of the deadliest contagious diseases of the time—polio, influenza, diphtheria and tuberculosis—and the influenza vaccine was the only one in wide use.

Those Florentines who knew the bittersweet narrative of this deeply troubled family believed that the father who moved into his new home on East Pine Street in 1946 or 1947 was more than likely a World War II veteran. He and his wife had found the perfect home to welcome the newest member to their family, an infant son. Joyful celebration quickly turned to mourning when the awful specter of disease came to call. The baby soon contracted a deadly disease that viciously attacked his respiratory system, making it more and more difficult for him to breathe, as his little body degraded and continued to waste away. It is believed that either tuberculosis or diphtheria was the foreign enemy that destroyed this baby's body and caused such devastation. How terrible this infant's pain and suffering must have been. Perhaps the pain and suffering of his

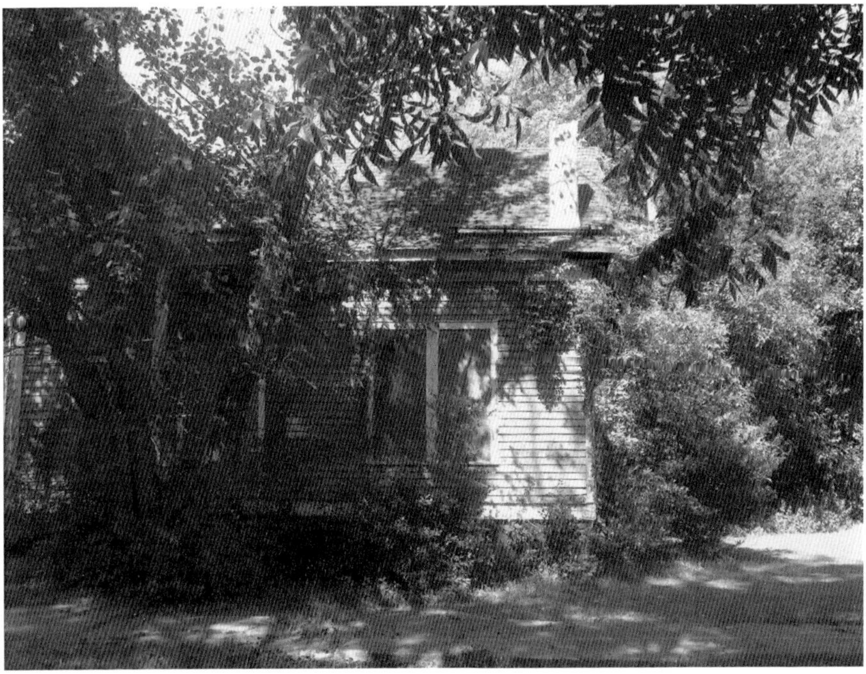

Helpless in shock and sorrow. *Author's collection.*

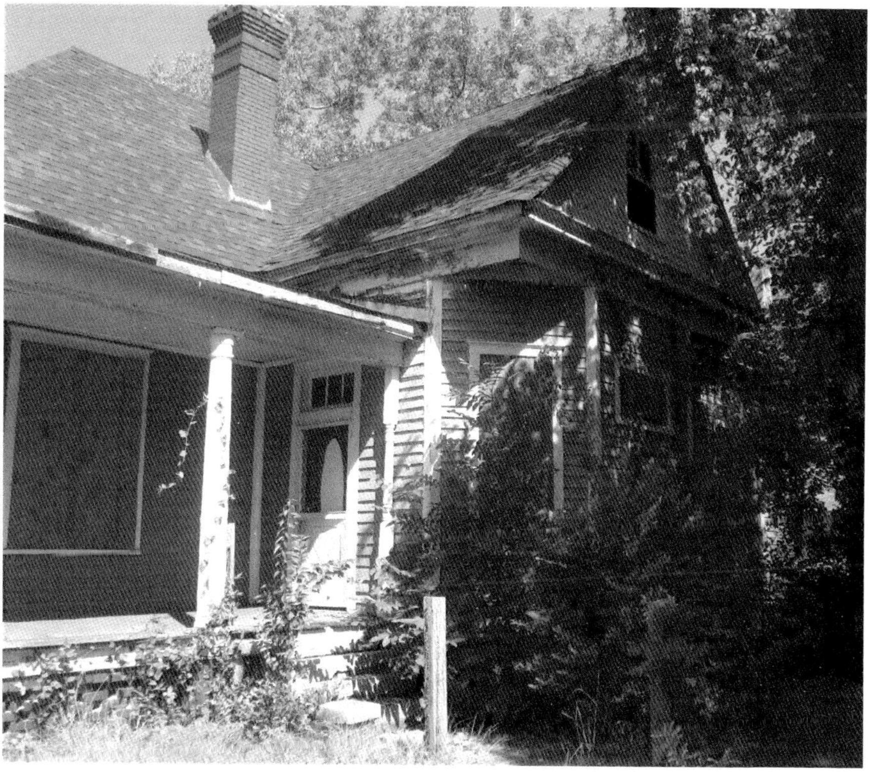

A crown of glory upon his innocent head. *Author's collection.*

mother and father, who had to look on in shock and sorrow as their son lay dying in their new home, was worse. They must have felt virtually helpless, as there was nothing they could do but wait to see if he might survive and anxiously wonder if there might be anything at all that could be done by medical professionals to save him.

One of the Florentines who shared this sad story believed that she has actually seen the ghosts of the grief-stricken father and mother in the moments of time that occurred soon after their infant son left his disease-ravaged body. The father's apparition was visible through a lower side window facing the street. He is wearing a suit and tie with his jacket unbuttoned. He is talking on the phone, and his facial expression is one of agonized sorrow. Perhaps he was sharing the terrible news of his son's death with a close relative or friend in this moment caught in time. The mother's ghostly image has been described as wearing her brunette hair loosely pulled up on her head and dressed in a nightgown and robe. She is holding a tissue or handkerchief to her nose and standing and staring blankly into an oval mirror on the wall of her bedroom.

Most Florentines who have been touched by this tragic ghost story and shared it have not seen the ghosts of the mother and father, but they have seen the apparition of the sickly baby, who is believed to have died in his crib while at home. You may also see the ghost of his disease-stricken face and body that appears to rise above his bedroom window near the side entrance if you pause to stop for a moment while walking by this haunted home. Some Florentines believe that they have even heard a baby crying from this room, despite the home's vacancy. If you see the ghostly image of this dying baby and are able to continue to see without turning away in shock and sorrow yourself, you may also bear witness not only to this baby's pain and suffering but also to his ultimate release, as a crown appears to begin to glow and shimmer upon his innocent head.

15
In Murder

There is a boarded-up home on Lawson Street built in 1950 that appears to have been abandoned for many decades. It has been rumored that those who approach this home may hear an ominous voice warning them to go away, even though no one is physically present. If they stay long enough to observe the back window of this home, they may see a surreal scene unfold—even through a window that has now been boarded up—of a horrific crime that was committed. The family was murdered and never had a chance to say goodbye before their deaths. According to local legend, there were supernatural reasons behind this bloody crime and psychic clues that began with practicing a form of spiritualism and ended with a black-hooded robe.

Attempting to communicate with the dead became increasingly popular in the United States in the mid-1800s through the early twentieth century. This movement was called spiritualism, and it emphasized the use of mediums and seances to aid in the attempt to inquire of the dead. Many considered it a part of the bigger Christian revivalist movement. The sentiment in the South toward spiritualism was not nearly as enthusiastic as it was in the North. The period in American history when spiritualism was the most popular was also during the time when antagonism between the North and the South was at its peak. Spiritualism came from the North and was therefore automatically treated with suspicion by most southerners, even though most southerners considered themselves to be Christians. The translation of spiritualism into Progressive politics also was unacceptable

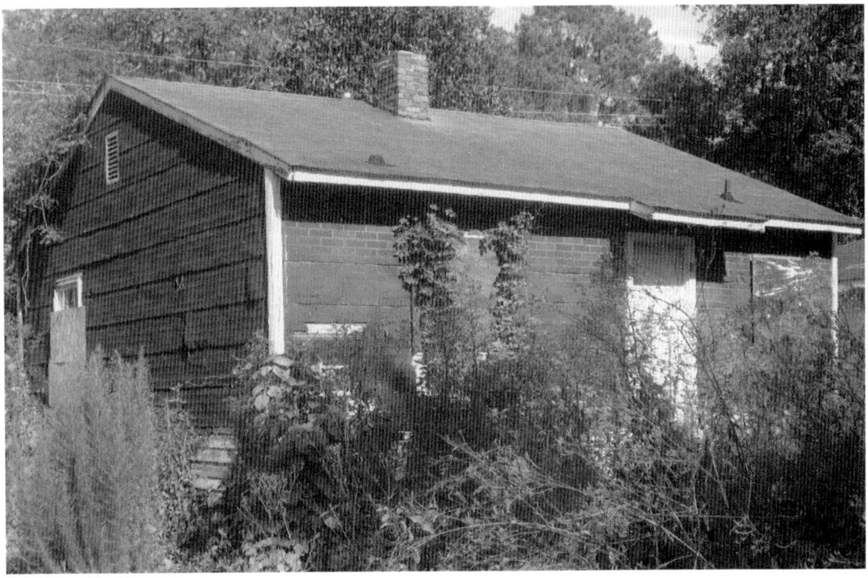

A surreal crime scene of murder. *Author's collection.*

for most Southerners. Some of the largest cities of the South during this time—Atlanta, New Orleans and Charleston—did allow for the exchange of new spiritualist ideas among certain circles or in local newspapers, usually in debate formats that did not completely accept or reject them.

Florence was only just beginning to lay its foundation and blossom and grow into its official incorporation as a city during the height of the spiritualist fervor. Today, there are no known spiritualist groups or churches in Florence. There are, however, a few Florentines who are known as mediums and publicly advertise their services. You may find these mediums advertising via the internet today, but back in the early 1950s, the most common way to publicly advertise was in the local newspaper. In 1950, the *Florence Morning News* included an advertisement for Madam Howard in its church section along with several local Christian churches. Madame Howard proclaimed that she was born with a veil and boldly welcomed all to benefit from her supernatural gifts without segregation. "Born with a veil" refers to being born with a part of the birth membrane around the head and face. Babies born with a caul are very rare and have been believed to be supernaturally gifted at birth throughout history. These supernatural gifts might include seeing ghosts, foretelling the future, healing and predicting weather patterns.

The phrase can take a sinister turn when the veil becomes a hood, particularly a black hooded robe. So has been the path of many who began to delve innocently enough into the occult, hoping to gain secret knowledge or special supernatural powers or even use supernatural gifts that they believed that they already possessed, only to discover that they had become completely overwhelmed or driven insane by what they had discovered or by what supernatural entities might have become attached to them in the process. Such has been the stuff of numerous horror movies and paranormal documentaries in modern American history that would seem to carry with them a clear warning to beware of the occult and, specifically, with anything that might be construed as worshipping Satan or the devil. It is arrogance and pride that have been the downfall of many, not only in the world of the physical but also in the realm of the spiritual.

The black hooded robe has been symbolic through the ages of death and the devil. The supernatural archetype of death as the Grim Reaper is depicted as a skeleton or a faceless figure in a black hooded robe. Many who have chosen to directly or indirectly worship the devil will wear black hooded robes as a part of their rituals to signify their souls' allegiance to the dark arts, including using supernatural powers for vengeance, harm, destruction, degradation and self-serving self-aggrandizement so as to better control and manipulate others through fear and intimidation. Beginning on this path of the dark arts may cause a person to feel so supernaturally powerful that they may believe that there is no limit to what he or she might be able to accomplish. Some may even believe that they have become gods and should be worshipped themselves. What most who practice these dark arts do not realize until it is often too late is that their supernatural power is only coming from being possessed by the devil, and they have no supernatural power at all themselves. If they attempt to break free from this possession, they may find that it has now become virtually impossible to do so, even through death.

According to local Florence legend, the terrible murder of this family was not perpetuated by a strange intruder. Even worse, these murders were said to have been committed by a family member who became possessed. A few extrasensory residents in the neighborhood believe that they have seen at least a part of this diabolical crime like a scene out of a horror movie from the back window of the home. They also claimed to have seen the face of the real murderer in this same back window with their own paranormal eyes. You, too, may even be able to witness this surreal murderer for yourself—demonically grinning in a black hooded robe—who is holding a teenage girl by the throat and observe that they are both covered in blood.

You may also be able to see the true face of the demon who possessed this man and provoked him to murder his family and himself. No historical records have been found to confirm with certainty who this family was and exactly what very dark and evil night that the devil surely won in this home. Perhaps if even one of these family members had sought supernatural help from one of the local Christian churches or even from Madam Howard, their lives would not have ended so tragically.

The stages of demonic possession include: manifestation, infestation, oppression and possession. Manifestation can be described as the first appearance of various demonic entities to test to see if you might be aware that they are there and what your reaction might be, if any, to them being present. These demonic entities may also disguise themselves to determine if you are able to spiritually discern what they are through this trickery and/or have any spiritual authority to require them to leave. Infestation could be described as demonic entities determining that they are able to remain in the space or territory that they have chosen. Oppression is one or more of these demonic entities attempting to attach themselves directly through

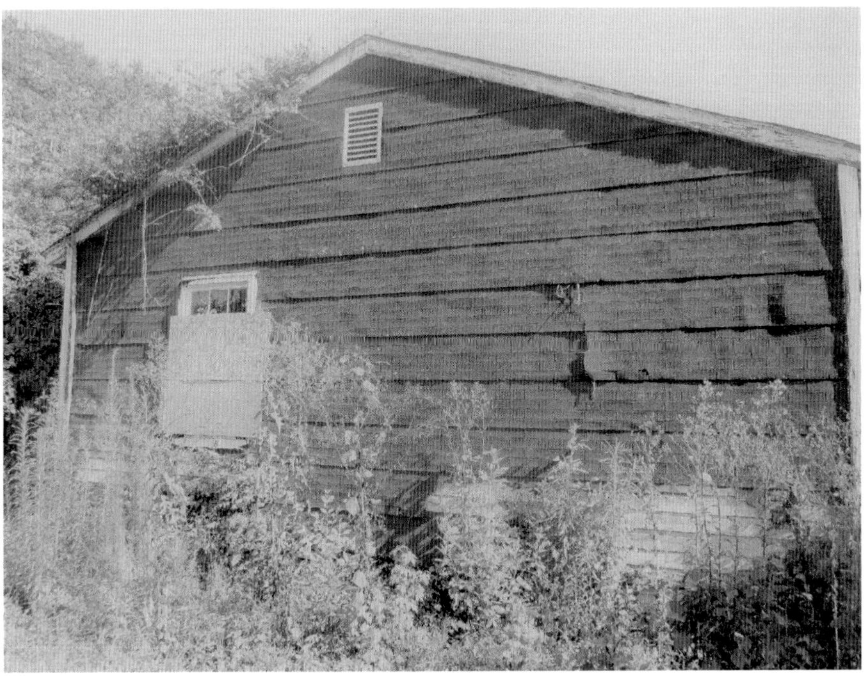

Locked in view. *Author's collection.*

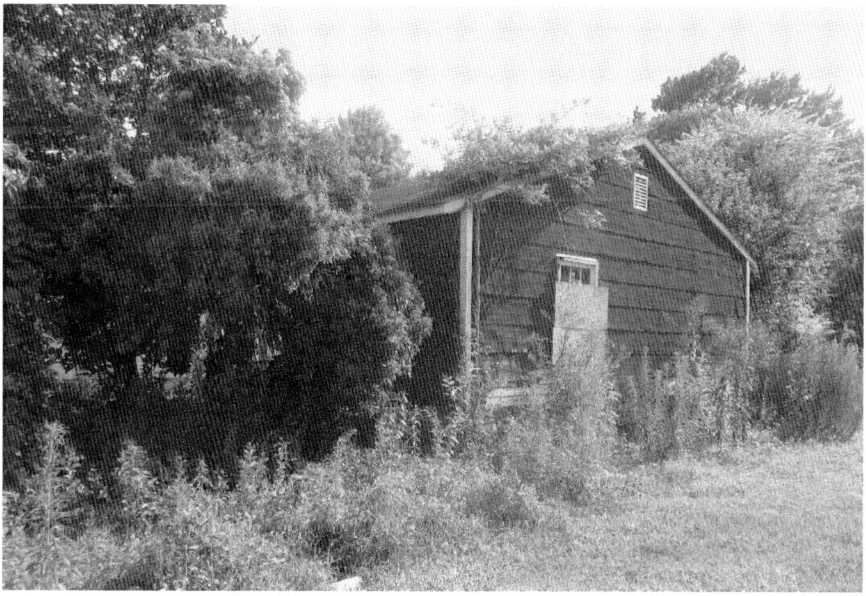

In a black-hooded robe. *Author's collection.*

the soul to begin to draw from your life energy in order to make themselves more supernaturally powerful. Many people who are being demonically oppressed have described feeling depressed; experiencing sleep deprivation; being supernaturally attacked; experiencing emotional, physical and sexual abuse; feeling like they were going crazy; and experiencing inexplicable outbursts of rage. Possession is the final stage: people have often described feeling that they are losing the will to live; that they already feel empty, cold or lifeless; feel that they are out of control; believe that their thoughts are no longer their own; are becoming increasingly obsessed with compulsively desiring to want to harm themselves or others; and are experiencing more and more frequent blackouts or significant changes in consciousness where they are unaware of what has happened while in these altered states.

Demonic possession, even temporary, can most certainly lead to violent crimes and death. Murder is not an uncommon outcome, even the murder of those whom someone once loved the most, even innocent children. It could be said that the most horrific crimes in human history were committed by those who were demonically possessed, though we may call it by another name today in the twenty-first century.

16
CAT'S CORNER

The mystique of the black cat remains hauntingly familiar not only to so-called witches but to any who have come under the power of superstition. Is superstition supernatural? Only if your mind convinces you that it is so, or so it has been said. The power of superstition is found in the power of the mind to believe. If someone believes that something good will happen, then the probability that this event will occur significantly increases. Conversely, if someone believes that something bad will happen, then the probability significantly increases that this event will occur instead. All belief must be based in the actual truth of reality that only wisdom can reveal in order for this logic to be so. Someone can be just as guilty of wearing rose-colored glasses and failing to protect themselves from real danger as being guilty of sabotaging themselves out of the good opportunities that they may have been able to actualize if they had only agreed that it could be so for them. Does the power of the mind require physical objects or creatures to make this power manifest? Is the power of the mind supernatural? Some say yes, and some say no to both. There is a local myth of an otherworldly black cat that appeared at some point after the 1910s, especially at dusk, at Cat's Corner in Florence.

The Black Cat Myth supposedly began in Ireland with the covetous tale of a black cat, a kidnapped girl and a mysterious woman who was able to succeed in obtaining anything or anyone that she wanted—if her desire or the desire of another was powerful enough to draw it to her. A business

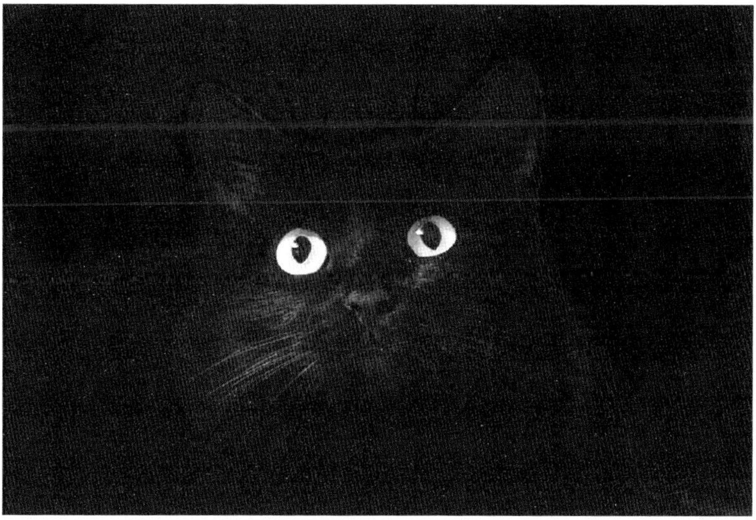

A black cat of fortune. *Courtesy of Pixibay.*

partner of the mysterious woman happened to see a girl out walking one day, and she became the object of his inflamed desire while he was in town doing business. He immediately inquired of the mysterious woman who the girl was and passionately insisted that he must have her for his own. Perhaps because of the implied riches that he would give the mysterious woman if she succeeded or perhaps because of the powerful desire that she saw in his eyes, she agreed to his request. When the lustful man began to doubt her, she confidently confirmed that she always succeeded in whatever she promised to do. She did, however, explain that her plan would only be successful if the girl walked alone past the location that she intended for her to be kidnapped because there could be no witnesses.

Sure enough, the very next day, the mysterious woman, who was also called a witch by some in her neighborhood because of her strange eccentricities, watched from her window until the beautiful girl left home to go visit her grandmother as a part of her daily routine. On this day, the girl did decide to walk with a friend—at her friend's insistence—because it was getting close to dusk. Undeterred, the rumored witch followed the two girls to see if the friend would travel all the way with the girl to her grandmother's home. The girls noticed the mysterious woman walking behind them. Becoming uncomfortable, the girl's friend insisted that they stop and let the mysterious woman pass, certain that she was a witch and that she was up to no good. The unsuspecting girl believed that her friend was being even more silly when, after letting the mysterious woman pass with a half-hearted greeting, her friend refused to walk past a black cat that appeared in front of them on the road after they had turned the corner. Her friend had now become even more spooked than before because the mysterious woman could no longer be seen walking on the road even though she had turned that same corner just a few moments before. There did not appear to be anywhere that she could have hidden that was near enough to conceal her in such a short time.

The frightened friend had become so anxious and upset that the girl told her to walk back, deciding that she would be fine to walk the rest of the way to her grandmother's house alone since she could see her grandmother's home in the near distance. This devoted granddaughter was never seen again. Although the truth of this disturbing tale was that the naive girl had been kidnapped by the crafty woman and her helpers when she passed by the location where they were waiting for her, the truth also was that this fate would have never befallen the coveted girl if she had not crossed the path of the black cat that day. No one knew that there had been a planned kidnapping of the girl. They only knew that according to her friend's account, the missing girl had crossed the path of a black cat—so, it became bad luck to cross the path of a black cat.

It is uncertain what year or even what century this myth first began. Although it is believed that it was the Europeans who brought this myth with them to what became the United States, not all Americans believed that the black cat was bad luck. In the South, another culture was forming that centered on certain African American beliefs that came from voodoo and hoodoo that black cats were good luck, particularly in gambling and with romantic success. The bone of a black cat could even protect someone from malevolent magic or make someone invisible.

Like the Trickster, perhaps what is found in the truth of the balance is that the black cat is neither completely evil nor good. In Florence, the black cat became linked to another local myth, the Falcon, during the late 1950s. Spotlighted in the *Florence Morning News* in 1959, contributing writer Eugene Fallon, or the Falcon, was reportedly able to make sparks come out of a black cat if he stroked it with his left hand at the stroke of midnight during the first night of a new moon. The Falcon also reported he was reading *Excursions into the Occult* during this time and was known for going ghost hunting in the cemetery at the end of Dargan Street on dismal and foggy nights.

It certainly would be a curiosity to know if the Falcon was aware of Cat's Corner at the corner of Graham and Pine Streets in Florence or if this might even be the same black cat mentioned by the Falcon that still haunts Cat's Corner today. Just when Cat's Corner became known as the haunt of this peculiar black cat though remains a mystery. What is known is that it would have had to have been at least some time after the 1910s because Graham Street was not added to Florence until this time. Had this very odd black cat once been the pet of a Florentine, or had this cat always been feral?

Either way, beware if you happen to see a black cat at Cat's Corner, especially at dusk. It has been said that this black cat may even begin to seem strangely familiar to you, with eyes that will unnaturally start to glow the more that you begin to stare into them, magnetically drawing you closer to it as if you were now in a hypnotic trance. If this mysterious black cat comes closer to you and purrs to be petted, you can expect that good fortune will follow. Do not be surprised if the cat disappears when you reach out to touch it. However, if this otherworldly black cat remains still and motionless, attempting to cross its path might not just bring you bad luck, it may bring you your death.

17
Mandarine Waters

The hulking abandoned relics of a motor lodge, restaurant and lounge on Palmetto Street in Florence appear to vacantly stare out at the cars and people who pass it by. A feeling that is sad and disillusioned rather than sinister seems to radiate from the premises for those who might endeavor to take a stroll through this part of Florentine history. Once affectionately called the Mandarine by locals during the height of its popularity in the 1970s, this location has now developed a new reputation since the turn of the twenty-first century for being haunted by ghosts and even a faerie spirit. The business interest for establishing this motor lodge on Palmetto Street all began with the Florence Regional Airport.

The Florence Regional Airport first opened the door to aviation for Florence in 1928 when local leaders purchased a 300-acre tract of land for this purpose. Expectations were high that this airport would help bring even greater recognition and prosperity to the still relatively new city of Florence and serve as another transportation hub for the entire Pee Dee region after the great success of the railroads. Mayor Herbert Gilbert was elected vice president of the South Atlantic Airport Association, which included North Carolina and Georgia, at the beginning of this banner year of flight, and he continued to advocate for Florence to have one of the finest airports in the country. It was during World War II that the Florence Regional Airport really began to take off with rapid expansion. During the war, the facilities were used by the U.S. Air Force as a training base, adding 1,400 more acres of land to the airport. Training continued with various groups such as the 52nd Pursuit Group, which was the first

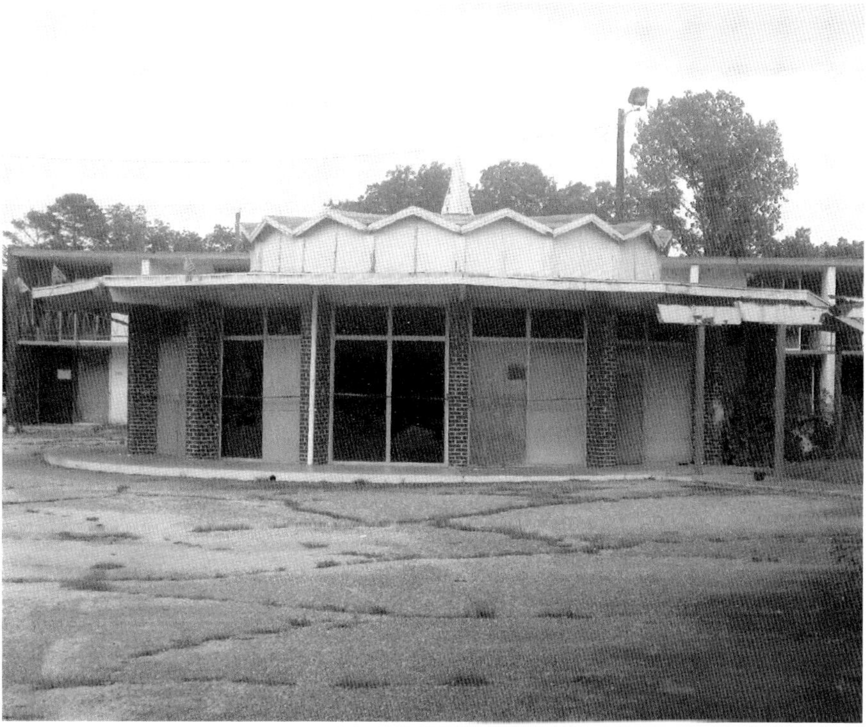

The hulking relics of the Mandarine. *Author's collection.*

group to begin training in 1942. After training by a series of troop carrier groups at this airfield, the 127th Army Air Force Base Unit was the last unit to complete training at this location in 1945.

A local businessman and World War II veteran named Tommy Griffin opened the Florence Air and Missile Museum in 1963 at the entrance of the Florence Regional Airport to honor other World War II veterans and showcase many of the aircraft and missiles that were operational during this war and the Cold War. Other exhibits included early 1950s and '60s military space hardware and even atomic bomb fragments from the infamous bomb that accidently dropped on the Gregg family property in 1958. It has been reported that at one time this museum was the most visited attraction on the East Coast between New York and Miami. The museum closed in 1997 after close to thirty years of dwindling tourist traffic, as tourists increasingly began to travel on Interstate 95 rather than Highway 76 to go Myrtle Beach.

Today, the Florence Regional Airport is experiencing a similar outcome and is currently only offering one scheduled flight on American Eagle to

Charlotte, North Carolina. Factors that have contributed to a decline in the number of travelers and flights are a sluggish economy, significant negative financial impacts on the entire airline industry and rising fueling costs. Delta stopped offering flights through Florence in 2010. Prior to this time, Piedmont Airlines stopped offering flights in 1981 and Eastern Air Lines in 1965. The Pee Dee Regional Airport Authority is a publicly appointed body that has overseen the development of the Florence Regional Airport since 1998, with nine representatives from Florence, Dillon and Marion Counties. There is guarded optimism from the Pee Dee Regional Airport Authority that the Florence Regional Airport will be transformed once more into a thriving and expanding airport in the near future.

The 1960s and 1970s were a different time for the Florence Regional Airport, with enough travelers and tourists on a regular basis to keep the facility really hustling and bustling. The FLO was offering multiple flights up and down the East Coast from New York to Miami. Those who came to the airport during this time were still able to enjoy the Florence Air and Missile Museum, a driving range and even miniature golf at this airport. In 1965, a motor lodge and restaurant were erected on Highway 76, also called Palmetto Street. These new accommodations were about a mile away from the Florence Regional Airport. Such close proximity to the burgeoning airport would most assuredly help guarantee steady business from travelers who would come to stay for awhile and enjoy some Florentine hospitality. This motor lodge and restaurant changed hands a couple of times through the 1960s and early 1970s and then became the Mandarine in October 1974.

A mandarine or mandarin is a type of citrus fruit that is grown from a tree native to Japan, Vietnam and southern China. Mandarin also is the language spoken by the majority of the Chinese population, even though it is technically only one of several dialects. The dried peel of the mandarin orange is used to enhance digestion in traditional Chinese medicine. During the Chinese New Year, mandarin oranges are given as gifts or used as decorations to signify abundance and good fortune. The owners of the Mandarine were of Asian descent, mostly likely Chinese. They moved to Florence from Myrtle Beach, where they had operated a restaurant called Hawaiian Kai. These owners were very aware of the potential business that could come from the Florence Regional Airport, making sure to mention in their postcards that they were located only a mile away—even offering free transportation to and from the airport. This postcard also showcased the sparkling blue waters of the spacious pool, which was surrounded by eighty-two rooms, with suites available. The grand opening of the restaurant and lounge was advertised in the *Florence Morning News* with a flourish, with the intention of attracting locals as well with the promise of something "new and delicious." Later advertisements also promised "good people, good booze, good music." The Mandarine did become popular with many locals, specifically being mentioned in 1978 by college students at the nearby Francis Marion College in a student newsletter as a go-to place for students to enjoy, describing it as "The Mandarine, for an Oriental touch."

The owners of the Mandarine motor lodge, restaurant and lounge most probably arrived to the United States of America some time during a great wave of immigration from China, Vietnam and other Asian countries during the mid-1960s through the early 1970s that began in 1965 as a result of the Immigration and Nationality Act. The legislation restored many basic civil rights to Asian Americans and made it possible for families to reunite with their loved ones. It is unknown as to exactly who these Asian owners were and why they chose to move to South Carolina. The Mandarine was in business for approximately six years through the mid- to late 1970s, but by the early 1980s, the Mandarine was no more. One fairly obvious reason as to why it went out of business was the change taking place at the Florence Regional Airport that led to a steady decline in travelers during this time as well as the opening of Interstate 95, diverting more and more travelers away from Highway 76/Palmetto Street.

A less obvious and subtler reason to consider was all of the social changes that were taking place in Florence during the volatile 1970s. The 1970s was a decade of great societal transition in the United States that was marked by regular cultural clashes between the new liberal hippie way of doing things and traditional conservative value systems that had spanned decades of time, resulting in many Americans who felt threatened and violated by these new terms that seemed forced on them virtually overnight. Florence experienced these cultural clashes as well, and not all Florentines were ready to welcome prosperous and prominent Asians to their city, especially those who might be communists or still "the enemy" in their eyes.

According to a former Mandarine employee, it was from this sort of bigoted Florentine that the Mandarine's troubles really began, more so than from the dwindling travelers. This former Mandarine employee and other local residents were convinced that they have seen the ghost of one man in particular who was a part of this bigoted group that was determined to see the Mandarine shut down and replaced with a country western–themed hotel and bar instead by whatever means necessary, including the deportation of Asian workers from the Mandarine. These Florence residents were uncertain if the mean-spirited man died at this location. This former Mandarine employee also was sure that he had seen the ghost of one of the female motel housekeepers who was deported still walking along the bottom row of motel rooms on the left side of this haunted complex when facing it from the road. Perhaps she came back to haunt the only place where she had ever found happiness, even as a humble housekeeper, the only place she had ever found any personal freedom, at least for a little while.

The most well-known sighting of the so-called country western ghost points to one spot in particular that may draw your attention if you walk straight past the restaurant and lounge toward the back rows of the motel rooms. Your eyes may be drawn to look up to a second-floor room in the center of the rows as if sensing that this room at least is still occupied, with someone or something that is able to stare right back at you. Witnesses believe that they saw the surreal image of a middle-aged man with dark, longish hair, a receding hairline and a thick handlebar mustache standing in the doorway of this hotel room with his arms crossed, dressed in distinctly country western attire, with a sullen, unfriendly and suspicious look in his eyes. Did this man die in this room? Was he someone who was at least partly responsible for shutting down the Mandarine, by whatever means necessary, so that he could have what he believed was a more appropriately patriotic country western hotel and bar to replace it? Does he refuse to check out from what might be his favorite room, even from beyond the grave?

Another aspect of the cultural changes of the 1970s that was believed to have contributed to the downfall of the Mandarine was the change in what was considered socially acceptable behavior. The first owners of the motor lodge and restaurant had a family-oriented establishment that catered to married couples with children who were traveling. By the late 1970s, the sparkling-blue centerpiece of a swimming pool that had once attracted children to frolic and swim had now become filled with mostly single men and bikini-clad young women who were increasingly enjoying the flirty fun and lurid excitement of reckless uninhibited freedom and the perfect place to party the days and nights away, with easy access to sex, alcohol and music, even regular live performances with no cover charge. The Mandarine had developed a very different reputation than what it might have once desired, but perhaps there was still a certain naïveté, even an unfortunate cultural misunderstanding of the trouble that this chaotic change of clientele could bring. Within two more years, the Mandarine was indeed briefly replaced by a seedy country western hotel and bar that quickly became known among certain circles as a hangout for prostitutes, drug addicts and criminals who

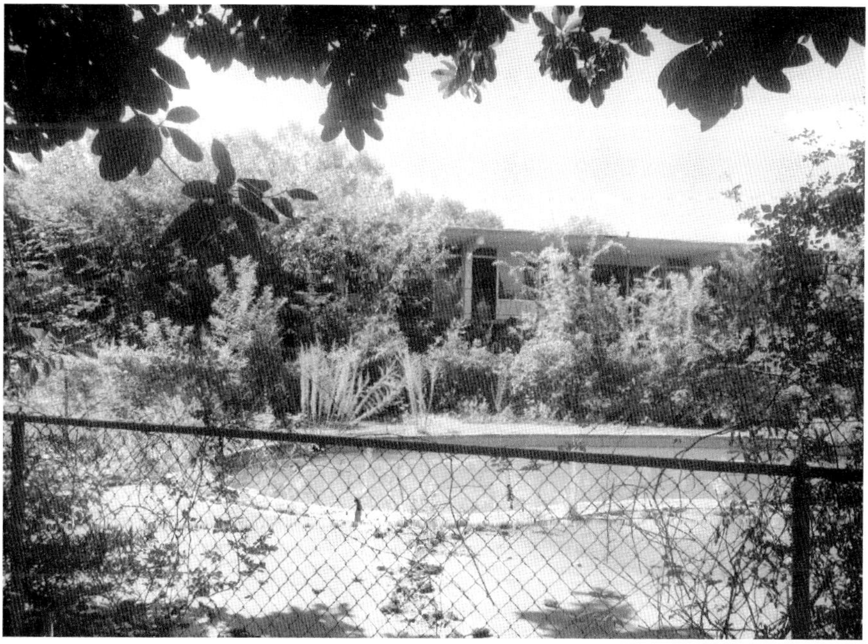

Mandarine waters of hope. *Author's collection.*

also liked to party the days and nights away, but in a much more hardcore and pornographic way, before it was closed down.

One Florence resident claimed that she even saw a faerie at this haunted location. She believed it might be keeping watch over or even guarding the pool. She affirmed that this feminine faerie can be observed among the wild greenery that is growing around a part of the second-floor balcony that overlooks the pool. This regal faerie is further described as sitting upon a throne, with a surreal castle from another dimension that reflects and shimmers in the window of the second-floor motel room directly behind. Asian folklore would seem to support this Florence resident's belief because there are faeries who are attributed with the qualities of being motherly caregivers and enjoying fruit.

The pool here has shrunken quite considerably from the grand size that it had once been. It is now filled with tears of sadness it would seem, instead of the sparkling waters of joy that it had once known. There is a glimmer of hope that remains as it still shines though from the almost magical wonder of a healthy and lushly green mandarin orange tree that still bears fruit next to this almost forgotten pool.

18

CALLING FROM THE OTHER SIDE

There has been rumored to be at least one known incidence of EVP in Florence, believed to have started during the 1980s. It was a regular landline telephone that became a spirit phone for an entity that attempted to continue to make phone calls from the other side in an effort to communicate with anyone who might pick up the phone of the closest nearby store to his home. How did this spirit accomplish such a feat of dialing a phone number from his own home telephone? So-called mainstream science still has yet to explain how such an event could actually occur, too often seeking to dismiss such paranormal events as impossible rather than just simply concluding that it is a mystery that remains unsolved.

The first concept of a telephone was like the children's toy of two tin cans or paper cups connected with string. The cans or cups capture sounds from the air, and the string transmits those sounds back and forth between them from a distance. Alexander Graham Bell has been credited with inventing the first practical telephone in 1876. However, there were many pioneers who came before him who helped lay the groundwork that Bell used as his foundation for mass communication. Such successful experiments in telecommunication by these pioneers began as early as 1833, when Carl Friedrich Gauss and Wilhelm Eduard Weber of Germany invented the world's first electromagnetic telegraph.

Most people know Thomas Edison as the inventor of the record player and the light bulb, but many do not know of his great interest in expanding his work in telecommunication to invent a telephone that would make it possible to communicate with the dead or, as he described his scientific endeavor, "personalities who have left the earth." It was in 1920, eleven years before his own death in 1931, that Edison publicly expressed this interest in *American Magazine.* He called his invention a spirit phone and stated that he had been working on this invention for quite some time. He expressed that his spirit phone would not function by "any occult, mystifying, mysterious, or weird means, employed by so-called 'mediums', but by scientific methods." At this time, despite Edison's stellar reputation, he reportedly shocked the public or was not taken seriously when he openly shared his desire to invent a spirit phone. Edison was unsuccessful before his passing in crossing this new frontier of communication. However, like the pioneers who first gave inspiration and laid the groundwork for Alexander Graham Bell to invent a telephone for practical use, Edison may have laid the foundation of inspiration after all for the invention of a spirit phone or a spirit box.

Today, Thomas Edison's vision for inventing a spirit phone may have been realized with Steve Huff's invention in 2015 of a spirit box he calls the Portal. Huff sought to perfect his invention, specifically by reducing static and improving the clarity of the spiritual communication that is being received. He now has an even better model that he calls the Wonder Box. Huff credits Stephen Hill and Frank Sumption, who invented earlier, more rudimentary versions of a spirit box that were based on modifying an AM/FM radio, as his inspiration. This kind of spiritual communication makes it possible for spirits to communicate through electronic devices and is referred to as electronic voice phenomena (EVP) in the field of parapsychology and in paranormal research circles.

The Florence ghost who has been rumored to have been calling from the other side is a man named Mr. Taylor, whose home is on Old Wallace Gregg Road in Florence. Store employees have claimed that they would pick up the ringing store phone to hear a large amount of static on the line and what sounded at times like a male voice attempting to speak and communicate with them. No one was able to clearly hear what the man was saying enough to be able to understand his words. When these store employees checked the caller ID, they would see that these very strange calls were all coming from the same phone number. The store employees knew Mr. Taylor very well and knew that it was his phone number. They also knew that Mr. Taylor was dead, and his home continued to remain unoccupied after his death. However, most of Mr. Taylor's personal belongings were still in his home, including his telephone, which his family was keeping in service at the time.

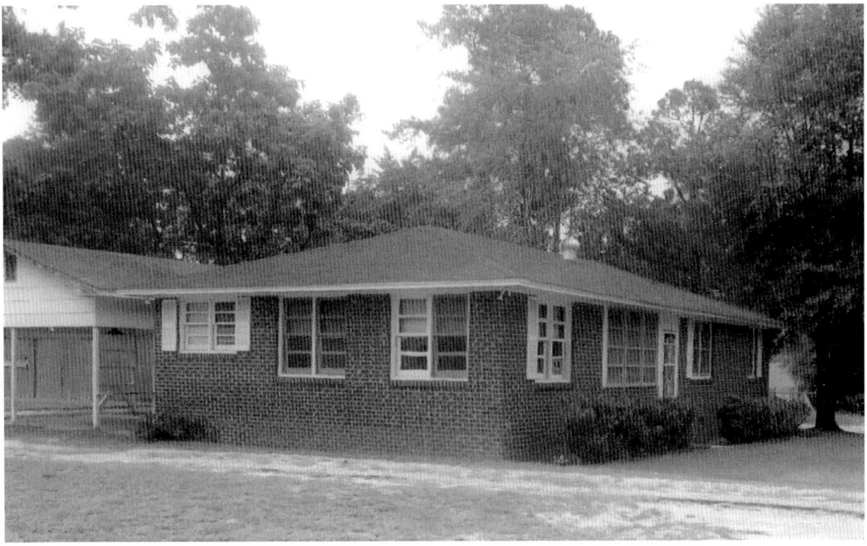

The Taylor House. *Author's collection.*

Store employees became concerned that perhaps there was an intruder who had broken into Mr. Taylor's home when they knew that there was no family member currently staying at his home. On several occasions after these upsetting phone calls, more than one of the store employees would go to his home to make sure that it had not been broken into. Every time that a store employee went to Mr. Taylor's home, the home was still safe and secure with no evidence of any type of a break-in or other disturbance, except for one piece of furniture that could be seen in Mr. Taylor's living room from an outside window on the side of his home. To the utter shock of these store employees, there was a rocking chair that could be seen rocking back and forth right next to a stand where Mr. Taylor's telephone was placed, a rocking chair with no one it, except for what could quite possibly be the spirit of Mr. Taylor.

19
Like a Bird

Bird appreciation through bird-watching and feeding became increasingly popular in Florence and the entire United States through the mid-nineteenth and twentieth centuries and on into the twenty-first century, first as a leisurely pastime of the wealthy elite and then more and more so among the mainstream American public. Prior to the twentieth century, birds of all kinds were often overhunted for food, traded and caged for entertainment and even for fashion. The invention and perfection of binoculars by the 1890s enhanced the ability of people to view birds much more closely. This intimate study of birds revealed their significant value to farmers for their better crop yields and for all who desired to keep their yards and gardens beautiful.

There was a local woman who apparently enjoyed bird-watching in Florence so much that some Florentines shared the quaint if not somewhat bizarre ghost story of the "Bird Lady." The Bird Lady is said to have been living in Florence during the first peak of popularity for American bird-watching, which is confirmed by the clothing that she is wearing when her apparition appears on what is now Chase Street. Those who have seen her ghost described that she is wearing a long lace dress with slight ruffles and puffed sleeves in its design, a style that was very popular in the late 1800s. She is further described as having chosen a lighter, summer variation of this style to wear for what may have been her favorite time of the year to commune with her beloved birds—she might also be seen sitting in a chair with a pair of binoculars in her lap.

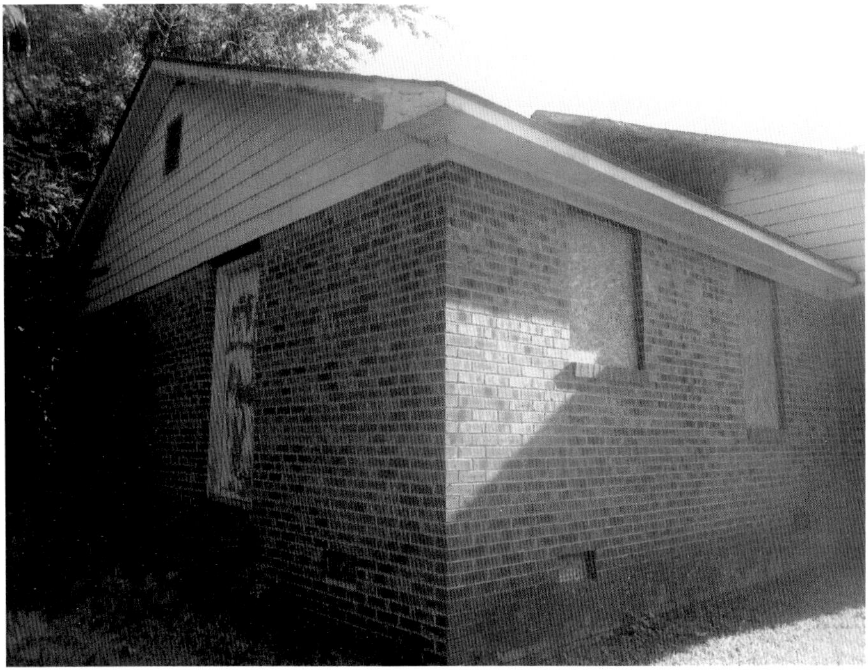

Bird-watching in Florence. *Author's collection.*

Perhaps the Bird Lady greatly admired another woman of her time, Florence Merriam Bailey, who was instrumental in helping to change the way birds were treated with her passionate bird preservationist movement. Florence's book *Birds Through an Opera Glass* was published in 1890 and has been credited as the first illustrated bird-watching field guide in the modern tradition. Her second book, *Birds of Village and Field*, was published in 1898 and significantly contributed to assimilating bird-watching and feeding into mainstream American culture. Another key component that led to a more enlightened view of birds was a farmers' bulletin written by Professor F.E.L. Beal that was published by the U.S. Department of Agriculture in 1897 titled "Some Common Birds in Their Relation to Agriculture." This bulletin helped to explain the practical value of birds to the American farmer and gave a justification for their need to respect and protect them. These combined efforts of the bird preservationist and appreciation movement victoriously led to the passing of the Lacey Act in 1900, which made it a criminal offense to illegally trade birds and other wildlife in the United States. The Migratory Bird Treaty Act of

1918 expanded this protection of American birds migrating between the United States and Great Britain, acting on behalf of Canada. This law made it illegal without a waiver to hunt, capture, kill or sell over eight hundred species of migratory birds and included protection for their eggs, feathers and nests.

Bird-watching was a hobby that did become increasingly popular during the 1800s in the South, with plenty of vast landscapes of trees and other greenery to naturally attract birds of all kinds. The mild winters in the South were an added attraction as well for migratory birds and bird aficionados alike. Plantation owners and their families in particular would sometimes include bird-watching as a part of their leisurely activities. Some South Carolina plantations that became known for their variety of bird species include Dixie, Mansfield, Magnolia and Vereen Plantations. A South Carolinian named John Bachman became a significant collaborator of John Audubon's during the 1830s. They worked together on bird studies after meeting each other in Charleston, where Bachman resided with his family. Bachman published their findings in scientific journals after Audubon's encouragement. The Audubon Society, which has become synonymous in American culture with bird appreciation, was founded in 1898 and named after John Audubon. Audubon was known for his prolific artistic portraits that demonstrated his great love of birds in a collection called *Birds of America*. The development of an even closer friendship between these two families led to both of Audubon's sons marrying Bachman's daughters.

Bird-watching in Florence's early history was not quite as popular as it was in the Charleston area. However, the Blue Bird Tea Room, which was opened during World War I by the League for Women's Service to support American troops, did publicly recognize bird appreciation in Florence with its namesake. This tearoom and restaurant was located on West Evans Street and served meals to troops who were passing through on the railroads and also raised funds to give to the Red Cross. The Blue Bird Tea Room closed a year after World War I ended with its mission accomplished. By the early 1950s, bird-watching and backyard bird feeding had become mainstream enough in Florence to be mentioned in the *Florence Morning News*. A couple shared a somewhat frustrating yet humorous experience in one article about backyard bird feeding for the first time and learning what bird trays and bird feeders would work best to attract the kinds of birds that they desired and keep out the kinds that they did not want. As recently as 2017, birds were spotlighted in the local news in Florence when elementary school teachers in the area banded and released birds as part of a learning project about birds and migration to share with their students.

According to the local legend of the Bird Lady, she admired birds so much in the flesh that she even became like a bird after death, with a beak on her surreal face instead of a nose and mouth, adding a touch of the macabre to this spiritual bird woman in what might have merely been a very pleasant ghost story of timeless history. Some of the Florence residents who told this tale of feathery admiration believed that they even saw the ghostly face of this otherwise attractive brunette woman transform before their very eyes. Of course, the Bird Lady may not have thought having a beak after death was disfiguring at all. In an ironic twist that also is strangely coincidental, a man named Rooster Young later built a home at this location on Chase Street in the early 1940s. It is possible that Rooster Young heard the local legend of the rumored Bird Lady and decided to build his home there for this reason. Rooster really was his first name—real enough to be listed in the 1942–43 Florence City Directory.

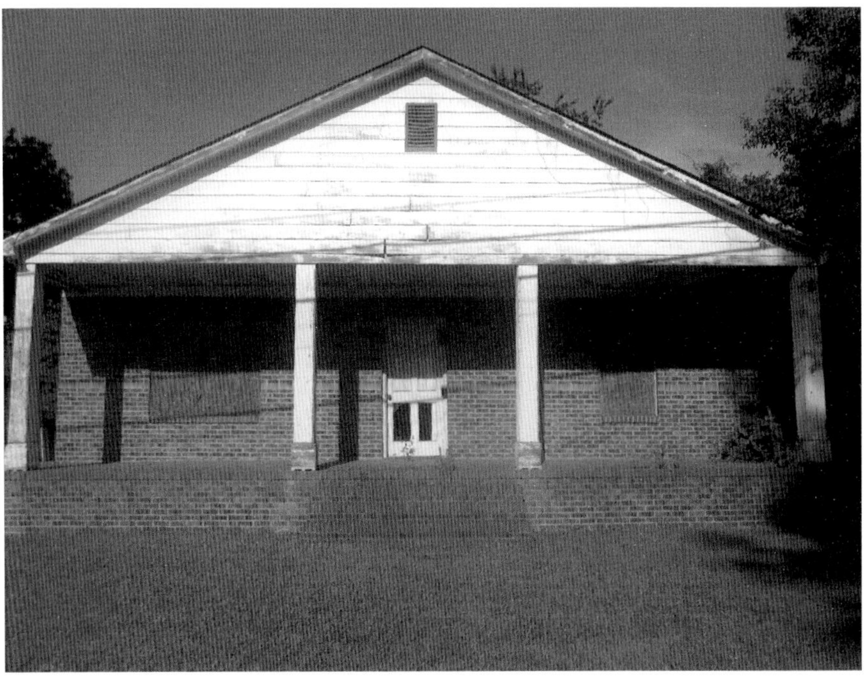

Rooster's house on Chase Street. *Author's collection.*

Perhaps spirits are like birds and are attracted to and reveal themselves only to those who will endeavor to put on their enlightened binoculars with the proper respect and appreciation that is required to begin to understand who and what they are and why they are able to connect and communicate with those of us who still remain in the flesh in a physical world. Those who embark on this spiritual journey will never be the same again, for the Great Veil will be lifted, at least in part, and the proof and continual confirmation will surround them that there is more, so much more after all than just the life we have known before death. However, there are some spirits, like birds, that are aggressive and territorial and are not as selective in who they reveal themselves to because they still believe that they have the right to remain in a specific place that no longer belongs to them. Those who genuinely seek wisdom will find it in how to victoriously confront such spirits and require them to leave.

20

TEST THE SPIRITS

Is researching the paranormal and participating in activities to understand more about life after death the same as being involved in the occult or in demonic activities? There are still many in the United States who may admit that the supernatural does exist but who also believe that God does not approve of human beings communicating with the dead. They may point to scriptures in the Holy Bible that they believe strictly forbid such communication, but only one scripture, in the book of Deuteronomy, seems to forbid anyone from making inquiries of the dead. Perhaps there may be so much confusion surrounding communication with the dead because the rest of the scriptures that are often referenced to support this biblical position that communication with the dead is forbidden include specifically mentioning people who have already chosen to be necromancers, witches, sorcerers, sorceresses, fortune-tellers, mediums, charmers, practitioners of divination, magicians, enchanters and interpreters of omens who attempt to communicate with the dead. Is it possible to communicate with the dead without choosing to follow any of these occultic practices that are strictly forbidden in the Holy Bible? Is it also possible that the dead may attempt to communicate with you without you doing anything at all to make any inquiry of them? The answer is yes to both questions.

Others may also support the position that communication with the dead is strictly forbidden in the Holy Bible by referencing scriptures that seem to indicate that once you are dead, you are dead, and there is no afterlife where you could be in between Heaven and Hell in a spiritual form. Therefore, the dead cannot communicate because they have been silenced, they are no longer participants in any way in this physical world and they know nothing now. So, if you think you are communicating with the dead, you are being deceived, because they must be demons disguising themselves as human spirits. This biblical position is problematic for several reasons.

Does physically dead mean that you are spiritually dead? Most people who believe in life after death would not agree that you are no longer able to communicate just because you are physically dead. They believe that you are still very much alive as a human being, just in spiritual form, without a fleshly body. There are also many believers who believe that there is a place called Purgatory, a spiritual plane of human existence that most certainly does exist between Heaven and Hell. Purgatory is the spiritual place where human souls may be required to go as they await the final judgement that will only come when Jesus Christ returns to the earth. They believe that this in-between spiritual place is also specifically mentioned in the Holy Bible as Sheol or Hades. Therefore, for all of these believers in the scriptures of the same Holy Bible, it is very possible to communicate with human beings after physical death. Some people also believe that these human souls may be lost for a variety of reasons that have prevented them from leaving this in-between place or that these human souls are refusing to leave and move on to the next spiritual plane of their existence and do still have the free will to do so until Jesus Christ's return.

So, are all of the spirits that a human being might be able to communicate with only demons? Two other scriptural points to consider are in the books of 1 John and 1 Corinthians. The first scriptural point to consider is the command for human beings to not believe every spirit but to "test the spirits." The second scriptural point to consider is that a Christian believer can be given the gift of "the discerning of spirits" by the Holy Spirit, which is the Spirit of the Truth. Why would someone need to test the spirits or be given a special supernatural gift to discern who and what the spirits are if they are all demons? Therefore, by any logical conclusion, all spirits that a human being might encounter are not demons as fallen angels.

Is there a difference between a ghost and a spirit? Ghosts are spirits who were human. Ghosts also are human spirits who look human in every way and appear as they did on earth, just without a physical body. Sometimes ghosts can move without limits; others can move within a specific space or may even remain completely static in one fixed location. Those who are supernaturally gifted with extrasensory perception may not only be able to see ghosts, they may also be able to communicate with them telepathically and/or empathetically, through thoughts that may be pictures or verbal words and/or through feelings. Sometimes a human being may be in a spiritual form and present after physical death but unable to visually manifest as a ghost and can only be recognized and communicated with telepathically and/or empathetically. Spirits are not always ghosts and not always human. It is very possible to encounter a spirit that looks somewhat human but the ghostly image has been significantly distorted in some way, usually by a demonic spirit that has attached itself to or possessed what had once been a fully human soul. Perhaps it was this type of encounter more than any other that occurred when attempting to communicate with the dead, and the experience convinced many that all communication with the dead should be forbidden. More careful spiritual discernment though would surely have clearly distinguished between a true human ghost and a demonic spirit that has only the resemblance of being somewhat human. Holy angels also are spirits that have been documented as communicating with human beings. There may be many other kinds of spirits as well that remain unknown to us because they have no contact with human beings in the flesh.

It has not just been the religious culture that has frequently sought to discourage and even forbid other human beings from communicating with the dead and discouraged and even forbidden other human beings from using their supernatural gifts. The secular culture also has sought to do the same. In secular culture, these kinds of discouragements are most often presented as signs in the field of psychology that a person is mentally ill or "crazy" if he or she openly expresses the desire and ability to use supernatural gifts to communicate with ghosts and spirits and even shares that they have already had these kinds of paranormal experiences. To be fair though, psychologists and other mental health professionals would not usually diagnose someone as being mentally ill unless the individual seeking help did not already believe that he or she was mentally ill and was looking for some type of cure to stop themselves from being extrasensory and supernatural.

For example, the belief that one can communicate with ghosts and spirits and/or has supernatural extrasensory gifts is usually translated in the field of psychology to a person being diagnosed with psychosis, schizophrenia, bipolar disorder or delusional disorder. A less mainstream psychologist or mental health professional may diagnose a personality disorder instead like narcissistic personality disorder or borderline personality disorder, where the emphasis in the diagnosis would not be on what the person was claiming to be able to see or experience but why they were claiming to be able to do so. These less mainstream psychologists and mental health professionals would conclude that the person was making these extravagant claims because of an extreme need for ego attention that would motivate them to present such a grandiose lie- and drama-filled alternate reality for themselves of having magical "super powers" that obviously could not exist. These same psychologists and mental health professionals might also conclude that people making such false claims were only pretending to seek help for more ego attention by increasing the number of people in their audience.

You do not have to be a traditional psychologist or a mental health professional to have essentially the same beliefs that someone who claims to use supernatural gifts to communicate with ghosts and spirits is either crazy or lying. Sometimes it might be fear of the unknown that could motivate someone to come to such an absolute conclusion or a bad experience with a person who actually was a fraud when someone had once been more open-minded and inquisitive. Some may believe in the supernatural and paranormal and may even have these types of gifts on some level, but they still fail to demonstrate the proper respect that is required to communicate with the spiritual realm in a beneficial and effective way and are therefore unable to use these gifts to their fullest potential. Exploring the spiritual realm is not for the faint-hearted or for fools who approach the spirit world as merely a new form of entertainment, to bully and to mock and still actually expect to have some kind of a positive spiritual experience, if at all. Instead, a fool such as this can expect to attract only the most unpleasant and undesirable of ghosts and spirits that will become greatly annoyed and offended by such arrogant behavior. However, it is unnecessary to bring physical offerings and gifts to show your respect. Remember, spirits are supernatural and extrasensory and they know your intent and motivation before you even attempt to directly communicate with them. Who they desire to communicate with is a person who is courageous, wise, empathetic, peaceful and, above all, humble. Wouldn't you?

Sometimes in a strictly religious culture, fear of the unknown might be compounded by feelings of jealousy that someone else is having supernatural experiences that reveal a deeper spiritual relationship with God that they have never experienced and might lead them to the same definitive conclusion that someone must be crazy, lying or just evil in some way and in league with the devil to make such an outrageous claim that they have supernatural gifts and can communicate with the spirit world. However, those who claim to believe in the words of the Holy Bible as truth have a difficult time supporting such a definitive conclusion when this document repeatedly describes supernatural experience after supernatural experience to support the opposite conclusion that we should expect as human beings to be able to be supernaturally gifted in some way to then be supernaturally empowered to regularly communicate with the spiritual realm. One popular defense of this definitive conclusion within the religious community is the "that was then, this is now" argument that God only allowed for such miracles, supernatural gifts and otherworldly experiences for a certain period of time that ended when the last words were written in the Holy Bible. They might further assert that if you are truly a righteous and faithful believer today, that should be all that you should ever expect and that should be all that you should ever need to believe in God. While it is true that faith should not require actual experience to support it, more importantly, it is also true that God is timeless and God is the same today as God was yesterday and will always be without the human limitation of time.

The Holy Bible may be the greatest historical document and resource that has ever been written for those who endeavor to explore the unknown of the other side of death with courage and wisdom. Fear and ignorance should never decide your destiny or your fate. When the past is alive, all things are possible.

Bibliography

Aftershock: Beyond the Civil War. Directed by David Padrusch. 2006. New York: History Channel, 2007. DVD.

Amadeo, Kimberly. "Stock Market Crash of 1929 Facts, Causes, and Impact." The Balance. Last modified April 5, 2018. https://www.thebalance.com/stock-market-crash-of-1929-causes-effects-and-facts-3305891.

Amtrak. "Florence, South Carolina." Accessed September 14, 2017. https://www.amtrak.com/stations/flo.

Ancestry. "David McGregor." Accessed August 8, 2017. https://www.ancestry.com/genealogy/records/david-mcgregor_4355787.

———. "James McLeod." Accessed November 13, 2017. http://freepages.genealogy.rootsweb.ancestry.com/~formyfamily/OtherMcLeods/JamesMcLeodAndMargaretBlakelyGordon.htm.

———. "Gregg." Accessed August 8, 2017. http://news.rootsweb.com/th/read/GREGG/2001-08/0997155502.

———. "Sanborn Chase." Accessed December 10, 2017. https://www.ancestry.com/genealogy/records/sanborn-chase_57554946.

Anderson, Thom. "Florence Little Theatre—A Retrospective." SCNow. August 24, 2008. http://www.scnow.com/entertainment/article_66ee1a41-a5ee-5902-b13a-c2e849ab6252.html.

———. "Industrial School for Boys: Pee Dee's First State Institution." SCNow. April 4, 2010. http://www.scnow.com/opinion/article_8f34de18-0d63-52a5-ac50-fad433d6b0e9.html.

———. "Old Directory Gives a Look at Florence in the 1920s." SCNow. August 28, 2016. http://www.scnow.com/opinion/columns/article_3b46ac5e-6c9c-11e6-aacd-db6630db09fe.html.

Any Place America. "Mars Bluff Firetower (AKA Wallace Firetower)." Accessed August 20, 2017. https://www.anyplaceamerica.com/directory/sc/florence-county-45041/locales/mars-bluff-firetower-1246539.

Architectural Styles. "Queen Anne." Architectural Styles of America and Europe. Accessed September 1, 2017. https://architecturestyles.org/queen-anne.

ArmyMechanic3rdID. "Florence-Ghosts," YouTube video, 2:12, February 15, 2008. https://www.youtube.com/watch?v=kdbWKZ-VHlY&feature=em-share_video_user.

Bibliography

Audubon. "John James Audubon the American Woodsman: Our Namesake and Inspiration." Accessed January 3, 2018. http://www.audubon.org/content/john-james-audubon.

Baker, Ken. "Historic Florence County Plantation Hits the Market." WMBF News. June 1, 2017. http://www.wmbfnews.com/story/35567607/historic-florence-county-plantation-hits-the-market.

Birdzilla. "South Carolina Birdwatching and Feeding Information." Accessed January 11, 2018. https://www.birdzilla.com/in-the-backyard/state-based-information2/south-carolina.html.

Bridges, Traci. "No Plans Yet for Old Florence Museum." SCNow. December 2, 2013. http://www.scnow.com/news/local/article_53ea82b0-5ba8-11e3-8f50-0019bb30f31a.html.

Britten, Emma. *Modern American Spiritualism.* Self-published, 1870. Accessed November 20, 2017. https://books.google.com/books?id=g_tZAAAAMAAJ&pg=PA435&lpg=PA435&dq=spiritualism+in+the+south&source=bl&ots=LZB5n8dti8&sig=_a2Me42y6T9F4wfYaCCVIzqMfEM&hl=en&sa=X&ved=0ahUKEwjYu93sm4PYAhWFmeAKHbIaBAY4ChDoAQgoMAA#v=onepage&q=spiritualism%20in%20the%20south&f=false.

Bullard, David. "Jamestown." Historical Marker Database. Last modified June 16, 2016. https://www.hmdb.org/marker.asp?marker=37338.

———. "Red Doe." Historical Marker Database. Last modified June 16, 2016. https://www.hmdb.org/marker.asp?marker=37306.

Buzzfile. "South Carolina Youth Advocate Program." Accessed November 14, 2017. http://www.buzzfile.com/business/South-Carolina-Youth-Advocate-Program-843-679-3189.

Carolana. "Florence County, South Carolina." Accessed April 3, 2017. http://www.carolana.com/SC/Counties/florence_county_sc.html.

———. "A History of Florence, South Carolina." Accessed April 3, 2017. http://www.carolana.com/SC/Towns/Florence_SC.html.

———. "Overview of the 1800s in South Carolina." Accessed August 2, 2017. http://www.carolana.com/SC/1800s/sc_1800s_overview.html.

———. "South Carolina Railroads—Seaboard Airline Railway/Railroad." Accessed September 20, 2017. http://www.carolana.com/SC/Transportation/railroads/sc_rrs_seaboard_air_line.html.

———. "South Carolina Railroads—William & Manchester Railroad." Accessed September 20, 2017. http://www.carolana.com/SC/Transportation/railroads/sc_rrs_wilmington_manchester.html.

City of Florence. "About Florence." Accessed April 4, 2017. http://www.cityofflorence.com/about.aspx.

———. "The City's History." Accessed April 4, 2017. http://www.cityofflorence.com/about/history.aspx.

———. "Planning Commission Agenda." Accessed November 12, 2017. http://www.cityofflorence.com/docs/default-source/default-document-library/september-12-2017.pdf?sfvrsn=0.

Cobbs, Kendra. "National Register of Historic Places Registration Form: Florence Downtown Historic District." South Carolina Department of Archives and History. May 20, 2008. http://www.nationalregister.sc.gov/florence/S10817721023/S10817721023.pdf.

Cohen, Alexander H. "A History of the Jewish Community in Florence." Jewish Historical Society of South Carolina. Accessed November 21, 2017. http://jhssc.org/a-history-of-the-jewish-community-in-florence.

Cross, Rebecca. "Florence-Area Teachers Get Lessons on Catching and Banding Birds." SCNow. June 21, 2017. http://www.scnow.com/news/local/article_5b1d54c8-56e9-11e7-809a-57f0eaf0e5b7.html.

CSX. "History & Evolution." Accessed October 21, 2017. https://www.csx.com.

Dixon, Gale Harllee. "The Life of Florence Henning Harllee." *Florence News Journal.* Last modified October 4, 2015. http://www.florencenewsjournal.com/good-life/item/v-the-life-of-florence-henning-harll.

Dunn, Halbert M.D. "Vital Statistics of the United States 1946." Centers for Disease Control. Accessed November 12, 2017. https://www.cdc.gov/nchs/data/vsus/vsus_1946_1.pdf.

Dwight, Dana. "Friends, Community Remember Businessman Griffin." SCNow. December 26, 2008. http://www.scnow.com/news/local/article_f85b558c-c6fa-58af-a13a-276a21a39ad5.html.

———. "Lee Steps Down as Chairman of Drs. Bruce and Lee Foundation." SCNow. February 4, 2010. http://www.scnow.com/news/local/article_64fa4561-f6ba-5457-9c6f-3560834a953c.html.

Ells, Mark. *To Hear Only Thunder Again: America's World War II Veterans Come Home.* New York: Lexington Books, 2001.

European-American Evangelistic Crusades. "Satanism." Accessed October 29, 2017. http://www.eaec.org/cults/satan.htm.

Everhart, Max. "The Tragic History of the Pee Dee Community Center." August 14, 2017. http://www.newsandpress.net/the-tragic-history-of-the-pee-dee-community-center.

Field, James. "State Series: South Carolina." Airline Geeks. September 14, 2016. https://airlinegeeks.com/2016/09/14/state-series-south-carolina.

Find a Grave. "Clara Willcox." Accessed May 12, 2017.https://www.findagrave.com/memorial/88995921/clara-willcox.

———. "Col Peter Cheves Gaillard." Accessed August 11, 2017. https://www.findagrave.com/cgi-bin/fg.cgi?page=gr&GRid=7919240.

———. "Gen William Wallace Harllee." Accessed May 10, 2017. https://www.findagrave.com/cgibin/fg.cgi?page=gr&GRid=83256324.

———. "Jerome P. Chase." Accessed October 16, 2017. https://www.findagrave.com/memorial/88997373/jerome-p.-chase.

———. "Kloo Lawton." Accessed October 16, 2017. https://www.findagrave.com/memorial/142767531/kloo-lawton.

———. "Lawson Chase." Accessed October 16, 2017. https://www.findagrave.com/memorial/88997229/lawson-chase.

———. "Sanborn Chase." Accessed October 16, 2017. https://www.findagrave.com/memorial/142767393/sanborn-chase.

———. "Sanborn Chase Jr." Accessed October 16, 2017. https://www.findagrave.com/cgbin/fg.cgi?page=gr&GRid=142767647.

Florence City Council. "Regular Meeting of Florence City Council." September 9, 2002. http://meetings.cityofflorence.com/archive/meetings_02/meeting_sept_02.html.

Florence County. "History." Accessed May 4, 2017. http://www.florenceco.org/information/history.

Florence County Clerk of Court. "Public Records Inquiry." Accessed June 29, 2017. http://web.florenceco.org/cgibin/coc/coc.cgi.

Florence County Memorial Library. "Histories." Accessed April 29, 2017. http://www.libsci.sc.edu/histories/vts/epw27.html.

Florence County Museum. "The Story of Florence—Part 2." Accessed April 28, 2017. http://www.flocomuseum.org/railroad/the-story-of-florence-sc-part-2.

Florence Downtown Historic District. "Red Doe Plantation." Facebook. July 25, 2017. https://www.facebook.com/FlorenceDowntownHistoricFacadesDistrict/posts/1465608036851314.

Florence Library. "Florence Fire of 1899." *Florence Daily Times*, December 19, 1899. https://florencelibrary.org/wp-content/uploads/2016/08/FMN19.xlsx.

Florence Little Theatre. "History." Accessed May 10, 2017. http://www.florencelittletheatre.org/history.

Florence Morning News. "Advertisement for the Grand Opening of the Mandarine Restaurant and Lounge." October 2, 1974. 3, https://www.newspapers.com/newspage/68527512.

———. "Advertisement for the Mandarine." October 6, 1974, 39. https://www.newspapers.com/newspage/68528425.

———. "Advertisement for the Mandarine." November 14, 1975, 5. https://www.newspapers.com/newspage/69664681.

———. "Advertisement for the Mandarine Motor Lodge." September 29, 1975, 14. https://www.newspapers.com/newspage/69660589.

———. "A Date with Judy." March 1, 1951. https://www.newspapers.com/newspage/67336748.

———. "Death and Funeral Announcement for Sanborn Chase Jr." July 22, 1961. https://www.newspapers.com/newspage/67481437.

———. "Florence History: Jerome Chase." October 12, 1971. https://www.newspapers.com/newspage/68823714.

———. "Florence Regional Airport." February 7, 1928. https://www.newspapers.com/newspage/18122844.

———. "Grand Opening of the Florence Regional Airport." January 1, 1928. https://www.newspapers.com/newspage/18119788.

———. "History Lesson: Water Everywhere, but Not Enough to Fight a Fire." June 13, 1977. https://www.newspapers.com/newspage/68486324.

———. "Madam Howard Advertisement." October 21, 1950. https://www.newspapers.com/newspage/67210630.

———. "Vulcraft Corporation Strike of 1953." July 29, 1959. https://www.newspapers.com/newspage/66799279.

Florence Museum. "Lysander Piano Trio." Facebook. April 2, 2017. https://www.facebook.com/pages/FlorenceMuseum/116400265051639.

Florence Regional Airport. "History." Accessed November 29, 2017. http://www.flyflo.us/about-us/history.

Francis Marion University. "History of FMU." Accessed June 8, 2017. http://www.fmarion.edu/historyoffmu.

Gelbert, Doug. *A Walking Tour of Florence, South Carolina* (Look Up, America!). Hendersonville, NC: Cruden Bay Books, 2010. http://www.douggelbert.com/florence-sc/. Kindle.

Ghosts of America. "Florence, South Carolina Ghost Sightings." Accessed June 2, 2017. http://www.ghostsofamerica.com/2/South_Carolina_Florence_ghost_sightings.html.

Goldfinch Funeral Home. "Obituary of Madge DeFosset." Accessed October 5, 2017. http://www.goldfinchfuneralhome.com/obituaries/Madge-Defosset/#!/Obituary.

Goldring/Woldenburg Institute of Southern Jewish Life. "Encyclopedia of Southern Jewish Families—Florence, South Carolina." Accessed July 21, 2017. http://www.isjl.org/south-carolina-florence-encyclopedia.html.

Good Tuberculosis Men. Progressive Management, 2015. Accessed November 12, 2017. http://www.cs.amedd.army.mil/FileDownloadpublic.aspx?docid=5c14d2f0-eeb7-47e6-bde0-98ac850ecbd6.

The Great American Stations. "Florence, SC (FLO)." Accessed September 17, 2017. http://www.greatamericanstations.com/stations/florence-sc-flo.

Green, Lisa. "Major William Pinckney of SC." Genealogy. August 14, 2009. http://www.genealogy.com/forum/surnames/topics/pinckney/421.

Hacker, Debi, and Trinkley, Michael. "The Economic and Social History of Tobacco Production in South Carolina." Chicora Foundation Inc. Accessed August 12, 2017. http://www.chicora.org/pdfs/Tobacco.pdf.

———. "Indians, Slaves, and Freedmen in the Pee Dee Region of South Carolina." Chicora Foundation Inc. Accessed June 10, 2017. http://www.chicora.org/pdfs/PeeDee.pdf.

Hacsi, Timothy A. *Second Home: Orphan Asylums and Poor Families in America.* Cambridge, MA: Harvard University Press, 1997.

Hamer, Ashley. "Thomas Edison Planned to Invent a Spirit Phone to Talk with the Dead." Curiosity. October 28, 2016. https://curiosity.com/topics/thomas-edison-planned-to-invent-a-spirit-phone-to-talk-with-the-dead-curiosity.

Hansen, Drew. "Florence Firefighters Extinguish Vacant House Fire." WMBF News. February 9, 2017. http://www.wmbfnews.com/story/34464618/florence-firefighters-extinguish-vacant-house-fire.

Hayes, David. "Deadly Diseases of Past Reduced to Bad Memories." *Chicago Tribune.* November 16, 1986. http://articles.chicagotribune.com/1986-11-16/health/8603260778_1_polio-rheumatic-fever-yellow-fever.

Hendrick, Carlanna H. "Florence." South Carolina Encyclopedia. October 4, 2016. http://www.scencyclopedia.org/sce/entries/florence.

Historical Markers Across South Carolina. "Florence Depot (1852)." Latitude 34 North. Accessed May 19, 2017. http://www.lat34north.com/HistoricMarkersSC/MarkerDetail.cfm?KeyID=2119&MarkerTitle=Florence%20Depot%20(1852).

———. "Lawton-Chase House/Florence Museum." Latitude 34 North. Accessed October 23, 2017. http://www.lat34north.com/HistoricMarkersSC/MarkerDetail.cfm?KeyID=21-32&MarkerTitle=Lawton%2DChase%20House%20%2F%20Florence%20Museum%5B.

History. "Child Labor." Accessed December 20, 2017. http://www.history.com/topics/child-labor.

———. "Inventions of Thomas Edison." Accessed January 23, 2018. http://www.history.com/topics/inventions/thomas-edison.

Hotel Florence. "Our History." Accessed August 19, 2017. http://www.hotelflorencesc.com/about/our-history.htm.

House of Names. "Marr." Accessed August 29, 2017. https://www.houseofnames.com/marrs-family-crest.

Huff Paranormal. "My Story and What I Have Learned About the Afterlife." Accessed January 29, 2018. http://huffparanormal.com.

Ideal Funeral Parlor. "Atleene Pinkney Obituary." Accessed July 29, 2017. http://www.idealfuneral.com/obituary/Atleene-Emily-Pinkney/Florence-SC/551616.

Imbeau, Stephen. "Come on Downtown, for Great History, too." SCNow. February 3, 2016. http://www.scnow.com/opinion/article_3646b2c6-c9f4-11e5-b5ec-37656a47a8a4.html.

———. "Florence Health Care Is Second to None in SC." SCNow. July 10, 2013. http://www.scnow.com/opinion/citizen_columnists/article_6d6ae99c-e8e3-11e2-bedc-001a4bcf6878.html.

Immunization Action Coalition. "Vaccine Timeline." Accessed November 28, 2017. http://www.immunize.org/timeline.

Inflation Calculator. "U.S. Inflation Rate, $100 in 1918 to 2017." Accessed October 18, 2017. http://www.in2013dollars.com/1918-dollars-in-2017.

The Internet Archive. "1978 Vignettes from Francis Marion College." Accessed October 7, 2017. https://archive.org/stream/vignettes81978fran/vignettes81978fran_djvu.txt.

Jackson, Gavin. "Florence County Approves Red Doe Plantation Preservation." SCNow. December 24, 2013. http://www.scnow.com/news/article_17f409ee-6cbe-11e3-9d4c-0019bb30f31a.html.

———. "For Florence Museum, Home Is Where the Art Is." SCNow. July 13, 2013. http://www.scnow.com/living/article_9b8756ec-ec05-11e2-ac09-001a4bcf6878.html.

———. "Red Doe Renovations Underway, Many More Ahead." SCNow. October 3, 2014. http://www.scnow.com/news/local/article_fd34102e-4b59-11e4-b07d-0017a43b2370.html.

Jamestown Foundation. "About Us." Accessed June 30, 2017. http://jamestownfound.org.

Johnson, Kimberly. "Suit Seeks to Bring Change to Embattled SC Foster-Care System." Al Jazeera America. June 16, 2015. http://america.aljazeera.com/articles/2015/6/16/suit-seeks-to-bring-change-to-embattled-sc-foster-care-system.html.

Kasal, Forrest. "How Were Slaves Involved/Affected in the Civil War?" Prezi. May 27, 2010. https://prezi.com/j0r7oqyxqidd/how-were-slaves-involved-affected-in-the-civil-war.

Kearney, Paul W. "Burn Your Own Home." *New Outlook*. August 1933. http://www.oldmagazinearticles.com/article-summary/1930s-insurance-fraud#.WfnojmhSzpO.

Keep, Lynsey. "Causes of Death in the 1940s." Love to Know. Accessed November 12, 2017. http://dying.lovetoknow.com/Causes_of_Death_in_the_1940s.

Keiger, Dale. "The Rise and Demise of the American Orphanage." *John Hopkins Magazine*. April 1996. http://pages.jh.edu/jhumag/496web/orphange.html.

Kleinberg, S. J. *Widows and Orphans First: The Family Economy and Social Welfare Policy, 1880–1939*. Champaign: University of Illinois Press, 2010.

Know it All. "Florence: A Renaissance Spirit, Part 1—Early History." ETV. Accessed May 21, 2017. https://knowitall.org/video/florence-renaissance-spirit-part-1-early-history.

———. "Florence: A Renaissance Spirit, Part 2—Reconstruction." ETV. Accessed May 21, 2017. https://knowitall.org/video/florence-renaissance-spirit-part-2-reconstruction.

———. "Florence: A Renaissance Spirit, Part 3—Early 20th Century." ETV. Accessed May 21, 2017. https://knowitall.org/video/florence-renaissance-spirit-part-3-early-20th-century.

Legacy. "Obituary of Thomas Griffin Sr." Accessed December 1, 2017. http://www.legacy.com/obituaries/charleston/obituary.aspx?n=thomas-griffin&pid=121866770&fhid=4461.

Library of Congress. "The Surprising History of Bird Feeding." YouTube video, 57:38. July 29, 2016. https://www.youtube.com/watch?v=LROCddFBstA.

Magic Yellow. "Psychic Mediums in Florence, SC." Accessed October 28, 2017. http://www.magicyellow.com/category/psychic_mediums/florence_sc.html.

McCray, Shamira. "Come Celebrate Jamestown Set for This Weekend." SCNow. July 26, 2017. http://www.scnow.com/entertainment/currents/article_b7cc1fc6-725d-11e7-bfd3-b7ef8979450b.html.

McLeod Health. "McLeod Regional Medical Center Lives at the Center of a 110-Year History." About Us. Accessed November 2, 2017. https://www.mcleodhealth.org/about-us/history.

McLeod Health Foundation. "The Journey Begins." Accessed November 13, 2017. http://www.futurefocus.net/mcleod/picture_journey.htm.

Murchie, Michael. "The Stages of Demonic Possession." Exemplore. Last modified April 19, 2018. https://exemplore.com/paranormal/The-Stages-of-Demonic-Possession.

National Park Service. "Florence National Cemetery Florence South Carolina." Accessed August 10, 2017. https://www.nps.gov/nr/travel/national_cemeteries/South_Carolina/Florence_National_Cemtery.html.

Native Languages. "Legendary Native American Figures: Swamp Woman." Accessed April 30, 2017. http://www.native-languages.org/swamp-woman.htm.

———. "Pee Dee Indian Tribe." Accessed April 30, 2017. http://www.native-languages.org/pedee.htm.

Newcomb, Andrew P. "Bird Watching Is Strictly for the Birds." *Florence Morning News*, January 2, 1951, 7. https://www.newspapers.com/newspage/67335245/.

Open Bible. "Communicating with the Dead." Accessed February 3, 2018. https://www.openbible.info/topics/communicating_with_the_dead.

Otr HalloweenHolidaze. "Origin of Superstition: Black Cat." YouTube video, 13:20. October 30, 2012, https://www.youtube.com/watch?v=8drpfeejzhw.

Palmetto Trust. "Mission and History." Accessed August 31, 2017. https://palmettotrust.org/about-us/mission-history.

A Patriot's History of the United States. "American Heroes: South Carolina's Swamp Fox." Accessed July 5, 2017. http://www.patriotshistoryusa.com/teaching-materials/bonus-materials/american-heroes-francis-marion.

Pee Dee Indian Tribe. "Home." Accessed June 18, 2017. http://www.peedeetribe.org.

Perry, Joe. "Outlook 'Optimistic' for Florence Airport." SCNow. October 3, 2015. http://www.scnow.com/news/article_be074cf2-6a27-11e5-bd0d-f750a122dcbe.html.

Prince, Eldred E. "Tobacco." South Carolina Encyclopedia. July 22, 2016. http://www.scencyclopedia.org/sce/entries/tobacco/South Carolina Encyclopedia.

Psychics Hookup. "Sister Hope Florence, SC." Accessed October 21, 2017. http://www.psychicshookup.com/florence-sc/6098-sister-hope.aspx.

Psychic Universe. "Born with a Veil: What Does It Mean?" Accessed October 21, 2017. http://www.psychicsuniverse.com/articles/spirituality/born-veil-what-does-it-mean.

Raymond, Robert. "The Falcon." *Florence Morning News*, April 12, 1959, 2. https://www.newspapers.com/newspage/66787509.

———. "The Falcon." *Florence Morning News*, March 29, 1959, 24. https://www.newspapers.com/newspage/66786032.

Reports and Resolutions of South Carolina to the General Assembly. Columbia, SC: Gonzales and Bryan, 1915. Accessed October 11, 2017. https://books.google.com/books?id=mXluPJHMoCAC&pg=PA153&lpg=PA153&dq=sanborn+chase+1918+florence+sc&source=bl&ots=O7x4xzSA1e&sig=nhDR2.

Revolvy. "Florence Regional Airport." Accessed December 2, 2017. https://www.revolvy.com/main/index.php?s=Florence%20Regional%20Airport.

Rogers, Jamie. "Florence Regional Airport Undergoes Expansion." SCNow. April 11, 2009. http://www.scnow.com/news/local/article_cf1ac884-7dc5-5d4e-8577-f6d53eadbdfb.html.

Rogol, Beatrice. "Temple Beth Israel Then and Now." Beth Israel Congregation. Last modified March 9, 2004. http://www.bethisraelflorence.org/about-us/our-history.

Rose, Anne C. *Voices of the Marketplace: American Thought and Culture, 1830–1860.* Lanham, MD: Rowman & Littlefield, 2004. Accessed July 7, 2017. https://books.google.com/books?id=hXmKkyGelowC&pg=PA38&lpg=PA38&dq=south+carolina+coonskin+cap+1830s&source=bl&ots=nFGJsYEHY8&sig=zVzTMjwQFytt4ilFHt30NXP7nrg&hl=en&sa=X&ved=0ahUKEwjU6jB5v3VAhVFNiYKHShfBxoQ6AEITTAI#v=onepage&q=south%20carolina%20coonskin%20cap%201830s&f=false.

Russell, John D. "Florence Museum Officials Look to Past as They Open New Downtown Facility." SCNow. October 7, 2014. http://www.scnow.com/entertainment/article_d16a96d4-4e6f-11e4-9965-001a4bcf6878.html.

Schrader, Kyle. "Antebellum Spiritualism and the Civil War." Gettysburg Compiler. Accessed October 21, 2017. https://gettysburgcompiler.org/2015/08/14/antebellum-spiritualism-and-the-civil-war.

Sciway. "South Carolina and the African Slave Trade." Accessed July 2, 2017. http://www.sciway.net/hist/chicora/slavery18-2.html.

SCNow. "Dr. Frank B. Lee, Florence Medical Pioneer, Is Dead." May 6, 2013. http://www.scnow.com/news/article_b249a3ca-b6b9-11e2-94a8-001a4bcf6878.html.

———. "McLeod to Celebrate 110 Years with Plaque Dedication, Choral Symphony." November 3, 2016. http://www.scnow.com/living/health/article_41202c68-a1e9-11e6-93fd-eb95dc751f5e.html.

Silver, Alexandra. "Top Ten Terrible Epidemics." *Time.* Accessed November 12, 2017. http://content.time.com/time/specials/packages/article/0,28804,2027479_2027486_2027527,00.html.

Smithsonian National Air and Space Museum. "Inventing a Flying Machine: Triumph." The Wright Brothers and the Invention of the Aerial Age. Accessed January 29, 2018. https://airandspace.si.edu/exhibitions/wright-brothers/online/fly/1903/triumph.cfm.

Smithsonian. "The War of 1812." The Star-Spangled Banner. Accessed June 20, 2017. https://amhistory.si.edu/starspangledbanner/the-war-of-1812.aspx.

Soft Schools. "South Carolina Colony Facts." Accessed June 28, 2017. http://softschools.com/facts/13_colonies/south_carolina_colony_facts/2049.

South Carolina Department of Archives and History. "Florence Downtown Historic District." National Register. Accessed April 30, 2017. http://www.nationalregister.sc.gov/florence/S10817721023/index.htm.

———. "Florence Public Library, Facade." National Register. Accessed April 30, 2017. http://www.nationalregister.sc.gov/florence/S10817721022/pages/S1081772102201.htm.

———. "Red Doe, Florence County." National Register. Accessed August 2, 2017. http://www.nationalregister.sc.gov/florence/S10817721013/index.htm.

———. "Slave House, Gregg Plantation, Florence County." National Register. Accessed August 2, 2017.http://www.nationalregister.sc.gov/florence/S10817721015.

South Carolina Picture Project. "Atlantic Coast Line Depot—Florence South Carolina." Accessed November 1, 2017. https://www.sciway.net/sc-photos/florence-county/atlantic-coast-line-railroad-depot.html.

———. "Jamestown—Mars Bluff, South Carolina." Accessed July 12, 2017. https://www.sciway.net/sc-photos/florence-county/jamestown.html.

South Carolina Plantations. "Gregg Plantation—Mars Bluff—Florence County." Sciway. Accessed August 9, 2017. http://south-carolina-plantations.com/florence/gregg.html.

———. "Red Doe Plantation- Mars Bluff- Florence County." Sciway. Accessed August 9, 2017. http://www.south-carolina-plantations.com/florence/red-doe.html.

The South Eastern Reporter. Vol. 29. St. Paul, MN: West Publishing Company, 1898. Accessed October 11, 2017. https://books.google.com/books?id=TT9dhCdHXJMC&pg=PA246&lpg=PA246&dq=lawson+chase+florence+sc&source=bl&ots=3Y_O5o8QDU&sig=pdesbfk1.

Stephens, Lester D. "Bachman, John." South Carolina Encyclopedia. October 12, 2016. http://www.scencyclopedia.org/sce/entries/bachman-john.

Sweeney, Clare. "History Lives: Visit Charleston's Antebellum Plantations to Picnic, Explore and Learn." *USA Today*. Accessed January 11, 2018. http://www.10best.com/destinations/southcarolina/charleston/attractions/plantations.

Trust Companies of the United States. United States Mortgage and Trust Company, 1919. Accessed October 11, 2017. https://books.google.com/books?id=7StGAQAAMAAJ&pg=PA497&lpg=PA497&dq=sanborn+chase+1918+florence+sc&source=bl&ots=AwPJ6hxjS-&sig=5K1WW.

UNC University Libraries. "Atlantic Coastline Railroad Company Records, 1892–1963." The Southern Historical Collection. Accessed November 10, 2017. http://finding-aids.lib.unc.edu/04572/.

University of South Carolina Libraries. "Sanborn Fire Insurance Maps." Accessed May 2, 2017. http://digital.tcl.sc.edu/cdm/search/collection/SFMAPS/searchterm/Florence/field/sc/mode/all/con/and/order/nosort/ad/asc/cosuppress/0.

The USA Online. "History of the United States Industrialization and Reform (1870–1916)." Accessed November 23, 2017. http://www.theusaonline.com/history/industrialization.htm.

Vulcraft. "History." About Us. Accessed October 30, 2017. http://www.vulcraft.com/about-us/history.

Wagner, Stephen. "Edison and the Ghost Machine." Thought Co. Last modified May 5, 2017. https://www.thoughtco.com/edison-and-the-ghost-machine-2594017.

Wang, Ling-chi L. "Chinese Americans." Countries and Their Cultures. Accessed December 29, 2017. http://www.everyculture.com/multi/Bu-Dr/Chinese-Americans.html.

War Paths to Peace Pipes. "The Trickster." Accessed May 29, 2017. https://www.warpaths2peacepipes.com/native-american-culture/trickster.htm.

Willcox, Agnes. "National Register of Historic Places Registration Form: Florence Downtown Historic District (Boundary Increase)." January 9, 2013. https://www.nps.gov/nr/feature/places/pdfs/13000060.pdf.

Wikipedia. "Atlantic Coastline Railroad." Last modified May 19, 2018. https://en.wikipedia.org/wiki/Atlantic_Coast_Line_Railroad.

———. "Atlantic Slave Trade." Last modified May 24, 2018. https://en.wikipedia.org/wiki/Atlantic_slave_trade.

———. "Binoculars." Last modified June 8, 2018. https://en.wikipedia.org/wiki/Binoculars.

———. "Birdwatching." Last modified June 9, 2018. https://en.wikipedia.org/wiki/Birdwatching.

———. "Black Cat Bone." Last modified November 20, 2017. https://en.wikipedia.org/wiki/Black cat bone.

———. "Coonskin Cap." Last modified March 11, 2018. https://en.wikipedia.org/wiki/Coonskin_cap.

———. "Florence Air Missile Museum." Last modified June 12, 2018. https://en.wikipedia.org/wiki/Florence_Air_%26_Missile_Museum.

———. "Florence Augusta Merriam Bailey." Last modified May 30, 2018. https://en.wikipedia.org/wiki/Florence_Augusta_Merriam_Bailey.

———. "Florence Public Library." Last modified September 23, 2017. https://en.wikipedia.org/wiki/Florence_Public_Library.

———. "Florence Regional Airport." Last modified May 14, 2018. https://en.wikipedia.org/wiki/Florence_Regional_Airport.

———. "Florence Stockade." Last modified January 22, 2018. https://en.wikipedia.org/wiki/Florence_Stockade.

———. "Haitian Vodou." Last modified June 7, 2018. https://en.wikipedia.org/wiki/Haitian_Vodou.

———."Invention of the Telephone." Last modified June 13, 2018. https://en.wikipedia.org/wiki/Invention_of_the_telephone.

———. "Joseph F. Leitner." Last modified November 25, 2017. https://en.wikipedia.org/wiki/Joseph_F._Leitner.

———. "Lacey Act of 1900." Last modified June 20, 2018. https://en.wikipedia.org/wiki/Lacey_Act_of_1900.

———. "List of Fires." Last modified June 21, 2018. https://en.wikipedia.org/wiki/List_of_fires.

———. "Mandarin Orange." Last modified May 27, 2018. https://en.wikipedia.org/wiki/Mandarin_orange.

———. "Mars Bluff B47 Nuclear Weapon Loss Incident." Last modified March 13, 2018. https://en.wikipedia.org/wiki/1958_Mars_Bluff_B-47_nuclear_weapon_loss_incident.

———. "Mars Bluff, South Carolina." Last modified June 24, 2018. https://en.wikipedia.org/wiki/Mars_Bluff,_South_Carolina.

———. "Migratory Bird Treaty Act of 1918." Last modified June 15, 2018. https://en.wikipedia.org/wiki/Migratory_Bird_Treaty_Act_of_1918.

———. "Monopoly (Game)." Last modified June 25, 2018. https://en.wikipedia.org/wiki/Monopoly_(game).

———. "Naval Stores Industry." Last modified September 16, 2017. https://en.wikipedia.org/wiki/Naval_stores_industry.

———. "Peshtigo Fire." Last modified April 25, 2018. https://en.wikipedia.org/wiki/Peshtigo_Fire.

———. "Port Huron Fire of 1871." Last modified April 15, 2018. https://en.wikipedia.org/wiki/Port_Huron_Fire_of_1871.

———."Progressive Era." Last modified June 27, 2018. https://en.wikipedia.org/wiki/Progressive_Era.

———. "Seaboard Coastline Railroad." Last modified May 18, 2018. https://en.wikipedia.org/wiki/Seaboard_Coast_Line_Railroad.

———. "William J. Wilkins (Architect)." Last modified March 30, 2017. https://en.wikipedia.org/wiki/William_J._Wilkins_(architect).

———. "Wilmington and Manchester Railroad." Last modified December 18, 2016. https://en.wikipedia.org/wiki/Wilmington_and_Manchester_Railroad.

WMBF News. "Police Search for Three in Florence Co. Shooting." June 15, 2010. http://www.wmbfnews.com/story/12621084/police-search-for-three-in-florence-co-shooting.

Women History Blog. "Native Americans of South Carolina." Accessed June 27, 2017. http://www.womenhistoryblog.com/2008/06/native-americans-of-south-carolina.html.

Yronwode, Catherine. "Black Cat Spells and Black Cat Spiritual Supplies." Lucky Mojo Curio Co. Accessed October 23, 2017. http://www.luckymojo.com/blackcat.html.

Zarrelli, Natalie. "Dial a Ghost on Thomas Edison's Least Successful Invention: The Spirit Phone." Atlas Obscura. Accessed December 20, 2017. https://www.atlasobscura.com/articles/dial-a-ghost-on-thomas-edisons-least-successful-invention-the-spirit-phone.

Zeigler, Eugene N. *When Conscience and Power Meet: A Memoir*. Columbia: University of South Carolina Press, 2008.

About the Author

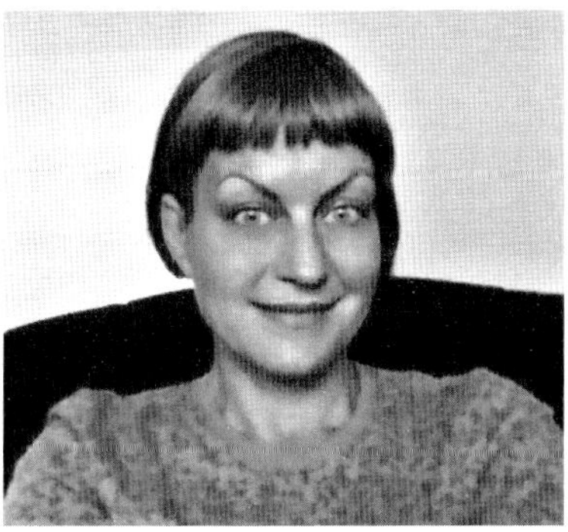

Heather lives in Florence with her young son Daniel. They enjoy exploring the amazing splendor of being outdoors in the beauty of nature's playground together as much as possible: learning, laughing and having lots of fun. Heather continues to enjoy writing of all types and going on new supernatural and paranormal adventures as well. Heather is currently developing her own curricula for a K–12 academic education program that includes the components of 1:1 tutoring, online learning, intriguing books of every kind and community-based experiential learning. Visit her website: https://hpbradley.wixsite.com/hp-bradley.